SKIING

and the POETRY of SNOW

JOHN FROHNMAYER

LUMINARE PRESS

WWW.LUMINAREPRESS.COM

SKIING AND THE POETRY OF SNOW
Copyright © 2020 John Frohnmayer

Printed in the United States of America

Front cover design and original woodblock print by Jessica Billey.
Find her on Instagram @jessicabilley to contact the artist, see more
of her work, and purchase limited edition prints.

Book layout/design by Claire Flint Last

Author photo by Tony Hayden, Aloha Studio, Lebanon, Oregon

POETRY CREDITS

William Stafford, "Once in the 40s" from Ask Me: 100 Essential Poems © 1982. 2014
by William Stafford and the Estate of William Stafford. Reprinted with the permission
of The Permissions Company, LLC on behalf of Graywolf Press, Minneapolis,
Minnesota, graywolfpress.org.

"Song for the Deer and Myself to Return on" from In Mad Love and War © 1990 by
Joy Harjo. Published by Wesleyan University Press and reprinted with permission.

Additional permissions on file with the author.

Luminare Press
442 Charnelton St.
Eugene, OR 97401
www.luminarepress.com

LCCN: 2020915711
ISBN: 978-1-64388-411-0

Leaving Town Alive:
Confessions of an Arts Warrior

Out of Tune:
Listening to the First Amendment

Socrates the Rower:
How Rowing Informs Philosophy

Sunriver: A Legacy

Carrying the Clubs:
What Golf Teaches Us About Ethics

SPIN! (musical comedy with Sila Shaman)

TABLE OF CONTENTS

Introduction

I kept telling everyone I was writing a book about skiing and mysticism. I got quizzical looks, oh-you-poor-baby looks, wan smiles, and head shakes, all of which were entirely appropriate. There are two kinds of knowing: the rational based on what we can verify, and the intuitive, which we can't. This book is about the intuitive.

But the intuitive can and does inform the rational.

Poet Donald Hall has written that anything that can be thoroughly said in prose—the rational—should be said in prose. "The everyday intellect remains satisfied with abstraction and prose; the poetic mentality wants more."

Ouch.

He goes on to declare that poems exist to say the unsayable and that poets are aware of the inadequacy of words because they spend lifetimes struggling with the unsayable. So, seeking that higher awareness, that perfect word in an imperfect language, that window into a world beyond, I have enlisted poets in the journey that constitutes this book.

Anyone who has gone to the snow knows that it frees us from gravity to the extent it is possible while still maintaining contact with the ground. The sensations of ripping down the Alpine slope or skating on the Nordic track may be different, but they share the singular virtue of allowing our minds and bodies to glimpse a world with which we are intimately connected, but can view only darkly.

I want to say that words
and wonder stay at odds.
Feel
what you see when you see it,
and the sight's within you.
Speak,
and it's gone.

—SAMUEL HAZO,
"The Time It Takes to See"

The Greeks knew that music is also an invitation to experience the hidden objects of our souls and that we are most alive in our most spiritual moments when we express gratitude, awe, appreciation, and humility. The world isn't about us; we are guests here.

And danger. Danger quickens the senses. Doing stuff that scares us gives us glimpses of who we are. Challenges are part of the world to which we are inextricably connected.

There are schools of thought that flirt with the intuitive, and so I have included superficial discussions of transcendentalism, Jewish mysticism, and Taoism, along with some ancient wisdom of the earliest mythologies. The inescapable conclusion that overcame me in putting all of this together was of the potential—no—the reality of loss: Loss of species, loss of habitat, and loss of life-sustaining water, air, and earth because of inattention to our planet's needs. Loss of our freedom, loss of our self-government, and loss of our ability to live peaceably with one another.

Then came the coronavirus, and loss of life jumped to the top of the list.

JOHN FROHNMAYER

So as the book goes on, my voice becomes more and more shrill. For that I make no apology. All of these—the rational, the intuitive, the earth and its health, our freedom and its health, and our lives themselves—are connected like an aspen grove. Life is short; time is short.

Play and hope and exhilaration, along with humor, will help save us if we just pay attention to what matters.

With arrogant humility, I invite you.

CHAPTER 1

The Edge of Day

The most beautiful thing in the world is,
of course, the world itself.

—WALLACE STEVENS, poet

I'd seen plenty of sunrises, but never from the windshield of a snow-grooming machine on the slopes of Mount Bachelor. Only the headlights of the Prinoth Bison, with its 400-horsepower Caterpillar engine roaring, illuminated the snow. We would not sneak up on the sunrise—if there was one.

The sky was clear as I drove to the mountain a couple of hours earlier. I saw some stars—no moon though. I kept looking toward the east, over the top of Bend. No sign of morning yet, but it was getting grey toward the top of Bachelor, and I could see its outline—the shoulders of the mountain—broad and muscular, sloping down into the darkness.

Next to join the awakening were Broken Top and the South Sister to the northwest—again just a hazy white outline. Now Tumalo Peak joined the show, or rather the anticipation of the show, because it was still dark, but to the east there was a hint that the sun was contemplating sharing its life-giving rays. A low-lying string of stratus clouds turned from grey to orange as a fanfare of the coming display, and the jet contrails formed a pink, cosmic cross.

It was in no hurry, the innocent dawn. The layers of orange and baby blue and pink heralded its arrival, yet Bachelor remained a monochrome whitish-grey, showing only its jagged contour. Progress, though: all three Sisters had come to the party. Now the first rays of direct sunlight hit the mountaintop, turning its soft snow, untouched by wind, pink and glorious and lumpy. This is what Homer called Eos—rosy fingers. The Romans called it Aurora. Summit had been groomed; at least there was one track ascending. The lift shed at the top was completely frozen—a block of ice as in a Siberian fairy tale.

And now, we needed a big drumroll, because the whole mountain was in sun, and the lumps had shadows, and the world was full of glory. Then it turned pink—the morning alpenglow that lasted only about 90 seconds and then quietly faded to white as the dark blue sky framed what must be the most magnificent of creations—the mountain and the sky.

> *No artist*
> *at his best could mingle pigments*
> *on a canvas to preserve this blaze*
> *of music from the drowning snow.*
>
> —SAMUEL HAZO, "Leafscape"

I kept thinking of Ferde Grofe's Grand Canyon Suite and the Sunrise movement that I had heard time and again at home as I was growing up (my younger brother, Phil, had a habit of playing vinyl records until the hole was elongated, which gave an antalgic gait to the donkey part in another movement of the suite). When I got home and listened to the piece; it didn't do anything for me. What I had just seen was wonderful in a whole different dimension.

What music can describe the sunrise since my purple prose clearly can't? Ravel's Bolero takes a full fifteen minutes to reach the climax where the trombones blare their glissandos like a skier flying down the mountain, but that's constructed and self-referential. Haydn's Creation starts out with God saying: "Let there be light." And there was LIGHT!!! The triple fortissimo chord with chorus, organ, and orchestra screaming full voice is meant to make the audience jump in their seats. That is showy but not what I just saw. And even the chorus proclaiming that "The Heavens are Telling the Glory of God" is just a reference, not a reality.

Morten Lauridsen's O Magnum Mysterium comes closer—the great mystery of the glory of our world in harmonies that are unusual and strangely fitting to the display of light and shadow that happens with a virtue all its own. I love that piece. Then there is Gustav Holst's The Planets. The Jupiter section bursts forth with exuberance, but...

So, now I want you to put down this book and go to your electronic device, preferably one with good sound, and google Sir Edward Elgar's Lux Aeterna as sung by the vocal group VOCES8. (Don't settle for any other rendition; VOCES8 is the best vocal group of which I am aware.) This four minute segment from his Enigma Variations is called Nimrod, after the mythological hunter, because Elgar's publisher was named Jaeger—the German word for hunter.

Elgar veered toward the mystical and mysterious in naming these variations, and critics and scholars have pondered who of his friends he had in mind for some of them.

The lyrics are: "Give them eternal rest, O Lord, and let perpetual light shine upon them." The vocal blend and the voices are extraordinary, and although I have listened to it dozens of times, I can never do so without a face full of tears.

The significance theory of emotions holds that our emotions tell us what is important. Forget your mind; it will try to fool you. Music describes what I saw on the mountain that morning better than any words of which I am possessed.

> *And you discover where music begins*
> *before it makes any sound,*
> *far from the mountains where canyons go*
> *still as the always-falling, ever-new flakes of snow.*
> —WILLIAM STAFFORD. "You and Art"

CHAPTER 2

No Rules

I couldn't wait for success so I went
ahead without it.

—JONATHAN WINTERS, comedian

In skiing there are no double faults, no technical fouls, no clipping, offsides, clock violations, or foul balls. No strikeouts, three putts, or shanks. Yes there is out of bounds, but anyone who skis past that sign is a knucklehead who not only is putting himself at risk but is endangering others who have to come to rescue him when he is lost or falls off a cliff. In skiing you make your own rules and set your own goals. There is no score—no winners or losers.

The lack of competition, for most, is one of the sport's greatest attractions. Yes, there are some safety rules, such as giving the skier below you the right-of-way, not jumping off the chair, not flying out of the woods without regard for those with whom you might collide; but for the most part, you can do whatever you want on the mountain, at your own pace and for your own fulfillment. That is what it means to be an amateur—a lover—of the sport and all that comes with it.

That love is a precondition, an enabler, for the mystical experience. Like love, one cannot willfully summon it up or easily explain it. It just suddenly appears and lingers or departs of its volition. It has an aura, a presence, a quickening of the senses, but it is in the realm of feeling, not language. Happiness, euphoria, wonder, sensual confusion—all words that are close, but no cigar. Can't explain it. Like performance art, you had to be there.

Singing, dancing, sex, and wine all can enhance spiritual and religious moments. Skiing is a lot like dancing except you don't have a partner, and lots of people sing to themselves as they are going down the mountain to help their rhythm. I am not sure about sex while skiing; seems to me the couple would have to be pretty athletic, and there is a lot of gear that would get in the way, not to mention cold buns. And wine is fine afterwards, but you don't want a skiing while intoxicated ticket on your record.

St. Augustine's famous pronouncement: dilige et quod vis fac—love God and do as you please—could be secularized into love skiing because it makes me free, which is a stretch but has the kernel of truth that freedom is both a fundamental human desire and, at the same time, a fleeting and constrained phenomenon. The poet William Stafford wrote that you can be free part of the time if you wake up before everybody else.

Ernest Hemingway skied the Austrian Alps in the 1920s, sometimes in the company of fellow writer John Dos Passos. Hemingway was taught by legendary instructor Hannes Schneider, whose Arlberg method revolutionized skiing (ditch the snowplow for the stem Christie and then parallel skis). Hemingway's goal as a writer of fiction was to use language so real that the reader would adopt the experience and make it a part of that person's own memory. He succeeded beyond most mortals in describing the thrill of skiing. Here are excerpts from his short story "Cross-Country Snow":

> the rush of the sudden swoop as he dropped down a steep undulation in the mountain side plucked Nick's mind out and left him only the wonderful flying, dropping sensation in his body...

> The snow seemed to drop out from under him as he went down, down, faster and faster in a rush down the last long, steep slope...He knew the pace was too much. But he held it. He would not let go and spill...

> Then his skis started slipping at the edge and he swooped down, hissing in the crystalline powder snow and seeming to float up and drop down as he went up and down the billowing khuds.

One of Hemingway's characters declares that there is nothing like skiing "when you first drop off on a long run"; the other agrees: "It's too swell to talk about." But Hemingway himself declares in "An Alpine Idyll" that he had stayed too long into the spring and was tired of skiing and of the spring sun. "I could taste the snow water we had been drinking melted off the tin roof of the hut. The taste was a part of the way I felt about skiing."

A Moment Ago

DEREK SHEFFIELD (1968 --)

you were following your steps
across the driveway, head bent
in the dusk toward one worry,
then another, and the day's last chore
in the plastic bag in your hand.
It wasn't a sound or a touch,
but something like the presence
of a memory that made you stop
and look up to find yourself
nearly surrounded by the dim
outlines of eight or ten deer.
And here you are, still, as if you've
stepped through the charcoaled
air into a scene on a cave wall
(the thin legs) where someone
long ago (the lifted, expectant head
and the tense breath) tried to bring you to life.

CHAPTER 3

Haunting

Always start out with a larger pot than
what you think you'll need.

—JULIA CHILD, chef

When I ask people on the mountain if they have had a "mystical experience," they usually say, "Huh?" That is, except for the hard-core ones who answer, "Every day!" It is the wrong question, son Jason tells me. Instead, I should ask how they feel when they are skiing, he says. "It just makes me feel so happy" is a typical response but not what I am looking for. A patroller answered: "I don't know if I would call it mystical but euphoric—I'm comfortable with that. Come to think of it, euphoric probably is mystical." And then his partner, also a patroller, said: "Mystical for me is when I am right on the edge of control on the super-steep and my focus becomes laser-like. It's just me and the mountain." Writer Kurt Vonnegut Jr. is on the same page: "Out on the edge you see all kinds of things you can't see from the center."

Then there are the skiers who tell me that they have seen people who weren't there, sort of like the Ghost of

Christmas Past in Dickens or the apparition of your dead grandmother. "Describe that for me," I say.

"How can I describe it? The people weren't there."

Another response is flashes of light, which brings us, as logic inexorably dictates, to why pirates wear eye patches. A young woman on the chairlift raised this issue on a sunny, long-shadowed December day, saying, without preamble, that there just couldn't have been that many pirates who got poked in the eye. "There has to be another explanation, and when we are skiing on a bright day like this and go from sun to shade, we can close our eyes for a moment to let the pupil dilate." I confessed to having tried it. It's terrifying at high speed.

I looked up the pirate thing and found a piece by Jim Sheedy, a professor of vision science at Oregon's Pacific University. Sometimes, when going from bright to darkness it takes as much as twenty-five minutes for the eyes fully to adapt. So it makes sense for a pirate, say one who is going below to plunder or fight in a dark hold of a boarded ship, to shift the patch from one eye to the other so he can see. Current-day naval officers who are relieving the watch at night wear goggles with red lenses so their eyes will be acclimated when they enter the darkened bridge. You learn stuff on the chair.

Riding the lift is also where I learned that the Pine Marten Lodge at Mount Bachelor is haunted. Apparently it is common knowledge. Toilets flush when you are the only one in the john. Elevators take off on their own, and the lights go on and off with no human impetus. And the howling. The moaning. Scary. "It is Bev Healy," a barista named Brian told me with assurance, referring to the widow of the ski resort's founder. I have to question this, because I believe the lovely lady is still alive. But, then again, in the realm of haunting, the rules are obscure. Her husband, Bill Healy, died in 1993 and is also said to be an unindicted haunter.

Prior to haunting the lodge, literally in another life, he was a champion skier and ski jumper in high school and fought with the Tenth Mountain Division during World War II. His unit ascended Riva Ridge in Italy's Apennine Mountains in the dead of night to overcome the Germans.

He stood on the very spot of the Pine Marten Lodge in 1957 when deciding that this mountain was the perfect place for a ski area. A pine marten, in case you wondered, is a member of the weasel family along with the badger, wolverine, and skunk. It lives primarily in pine trees, has semi-retractable claws, and eats squirrels. It is cute, agile, and able to withstand severe cold with its double-coated fur.

Mount Bachelor's ski area opened in 1958 and has aggressively expanded ever since. The Pine Marten Lodge, which is, predictably, at the top of the Pine Marten Lift, is a grey cement structure that slightly resembles an aircraft carrier. Lodges way up on a mountain are always problematic. It is not just the haunting. Skiers are there to ski, not sit around and eat and drink. Drinking alcohol, in particular, is a bad idea when you have to zoom down the gravity-enhanced snow afterwards—although as one happy skier put it: "Beer levels out the moguls." Another observed that his friend had frozen beer on his butt.

The lodge is huge with multiple levels. The top part is screened off and is highly underutilized most of the year. In the summer one can ride the lift up and have a meal there. The views of the Three Sisters and Broken Top would be spectacular if the lodge faced the other direction. It faces the summit of Mount Bachelor, with a bronze statue of Bill Healy pointing toward the top. He looks a lot like John Denver except that he doesn't have on the round glasses in the sculpture.

Bill Healy was plagued with a neurological disorder—probably Lou Gehrig's disease, ALS—toward the end of his life. With a life vector such as his, it didn't keep him from the mountain and from doing the things he loved. One day he was at the controls of a PistenBully (one of those monster grooming machines) while a Sports Illustrated photographer stood on the track to get a better view of the finish line. Bill fired up the engine, the machine lurched forward, and the photographer went flying off to a spectacular head-plant. I heard this anecdote from the photographer, who had breakfast with my son, Aaron, and me at Whistler in British Columbia. The photographer didn't think it the least bit funny, and in fact, had a few choice words about Bill that are not printable here.

Back to the mystical experience question. One answer comes from this anecdote told by Steve, a guy I met in the lodge where I was buttonholing people and asking obnoxious questions. He was skiing with his friends Dave and Linda at Snowbird in Utah on a pristine powder day. Dave and Linda, a married couple, have had a long-standing discussion about which is better: sex or powder skiing. So, they completed their first run of the day, snow flying over their heads, fresh tracks, whoops on every turn, then stopped to assess.

Steve: "So what's the verdict?"
Dave: "Sorry, Linda."
Linda: "What makes you think I disagree, Stud?"

CHAPTER 4

Transcendentalism

Direct your eye sight inward, and you'll find
A thousand regions in your mind
Yet undiscovered.

—HENRY DAVID THOREAU, philosopher

The transcendental movement, of which Emerson and Thoreau were primary exponents, flourished in nineteenth-century America as something of a second American Revolution. This revolution, however, was against dogma, custom, religion, society, government, taxes, and just about anything else that was thought to interfere with human individuality. The human mind is a fragment of the universal mind, and Thoreau, in particular, went to Walden Pond near Concord, Massachusetts, to shed civilization and commune with nature with the goal of looking inward and nurturing his spiritual independence.

The exponents are by no means unified, with some such as Thomas Carlyle (1795-1881) urging moral conscience and responsibility for one another and others such as Ralph Waldo Emerson (1803-1882) eschewing charity, or at least charities that were organized by societal groups of which he disapproved.

Nature for Emerson was the midwife that could deliver inward light. The superficial, as represented by society's institutions, just gets in the way of intuition and self-knowledge. The soul has a life independent of the senses, but nature, where our senses can be most acute and most instructive, can lead us to self-revelation.

Henry David Thoreau (1817-1862) wasn't quite as definite, allowing how our senses may fool us, but that they are helpful to see what is darkly visible in the world of nature. This is reminiscent of Plato's cave metaphor, where reality is reflected in shadow and is knowable only to the most enlightened. The vocabulary they created for this new way of thinking is a foreshadowing of philosopher Ludwig Wittgenstein's wordplay a century later.

Emerson described his own Saul-on-the-road-to-Damascus moment in the 1836 essay Nature:

> Standing on the bare ground—my head bathed by the blithe air, and uplifted into infinite space—all mean egotism vanishes. I become a transparent eyeball; I am nothing; I see I am part or particle of God.

Naturally the critics had a field day with the giant eyeball as well as the notion that essence was preeminent to existence. The Dial, a transcendentalist periodical, declared: "Great is the man whom his age despises." The critics are mostly forgotten, but Emerson and Thoreau soldier on in the American imagination, not because anyone is going to adopt their thinking wholesale, but because they have been so influential on so many who have changed the world, such as Gandhi, Martin Luther King Jr., and Nelson Mandela. Philosophy is like that: one takes a bit from this thinker and a bit from another and pieces together a worldview that works for a while. When it stops working, the process begins again; or more accurately, the process is never quiet—it is ongoing for a lifetime. It is ongoing for societal change.

Emerson objected to conforming to customs that have "become dead to you" because doing so "scatters your force." By solitude, one can touch the sublime. It returns the spirit of infancy into the era of manhood. Emerson uses the term "instinct" repeatedly to describe an intelligence that finds a unity between the material world and the universal soul. He describes it as "eating angel's food"—a wonderful term and a description of how to listen to nature and thereby discover the inner voice. "Only in the instinct of the lower animals, we find the suggestion of the method of it, and something higher than our understanding."

There is an urgency in the words of the transcendentalists. Thoreau famously stated in his essay "Where I Lived, What I Lived For": "I went to the woods because I wished to live deliberately, to front only the essential facts of life, and see if I could not learn what it had to teach, and not, when I came to die, to discover that I had not lived." It is a sobering thought for each of us. I sure as hell don't want my epitaph to read: "He neglected to live."

In his conclusion to Walden, Thoreau says he left there for the same reason that he came—that he had several more lives to live and couldn't spare the time. More urgency. But:

I learned this, at least, by my experiment: that if one advances confidently in the direction of his dreams, and endeavors to live the life which he has imagined, he will meet with a success unexpected in common hours. He will…pass an invisible boundary; …and he will live with the license of a higher order of beings.

Poet Emily Dickinson seldom left her room—hardly what one would call a wilderness explorer. But her writing was daring, and original, and inclusive of topics ranging from the serenity of nature to the ever-present specter of death. She was an explorer of her own mind, and as such, she fits within the transcendental movement although, were she alive, she might be amused to be classified as a part of any school of thought. Here is her reflection of nature as observed from her window.

Some keep the Sabbath going to Church

EMILY DICKINSON (1830-1886)

Some keep the Sabbath going to Church—
I keep it, staying at Home—
With a Bobolink for a Chorister—
And an Orchard, for a Dome—
Some keep the Sabbath in Surplice—
I, just wear my Wings—
And instead of tolling the Bell, for Church—
Our little Sexton—Sings.
God preaches, a noted Clergyman—
And the sermon is never long,
So instead of getting to Heaven, at last—
I'm going, all along.

CHAPTER 5

The Best Words

Poets are the unacknowledged
legislators of the world.

—PERCY BYSSHE SHELLEY, poet

Poets make extravagant claims for their craft: "Poetry explores the depths of thought and feeling that civilization requires for its survival." Lorna Dee Cervantes said that. "Everything is connected—religion, the body, politics, our relation to each other and all other living beings, the environment—it is all one vision and poetry is at the center." That's Marge Piercy.

Extravagant or not, these claims have substance. According to the poet William Butler Yeats, "rhetoric is the argument you have with others; poetry is the argument you have with yourself." A poem draws on everything the poet has ever seen, known, or experienced. It is the decryption machine for self-understanding. Poetry is a quest to make sense of the senseless, to plumb mystery, uncertainty, and doubt. Poet Jane Hirshfield uses the analogy of an ocean swimmer waving. Those on shore wave back, but the swimmer isn't waving; she is drowning.

Because the mystical, the transcendental, the self-enlightenment I am chasing here is so squishy and imprecise, I am including voices of poets whose well-chosen words may shed light on the quest.

Writing a poem is a solitary event, like meditation or prayer. It requires just the right word, the right cadence, the subtle nuance. Its stock and trade is the metaphor—the lie that is true. But poetry is meant to be read out loud so we can relish the consonants and vowels, the verbs and the adjectives, each chosen with precision. Poetry is language in its finest clothes; it is music in love with itself, and it is magic. It takes guts for the poet to lay it all out there—to embrace vulnerability so that we might better know ourselves. Marge Piercy says: "You never know when a poem will come to someone's rescue."

Here is a description of poetry writing by Mark Doty:

Yeats said a great and terrifying thing: "All that is personal soon rots unless it is packed in ice or salt." Of course the ice and salt he meant was the power of form, the preservative element of language which can hold a moment from the past, allow us to return to it, and allow us to give it to someone else. That element lets you as a reader enter imaginatively into the poem, be a part of it yourself, so that the poem becomes kind of a meeting ground between us. Art has that power. A good poem may begin in self-expression, but it ends as art, which means it isn't really for the writer anymore, but for the reader who steps in and makes the experience of the poem his or her own. Therein lies the marvel—something as small as a poem extends our lives.

Such a poet and interpreter of life was William Stafford, poet laureate of Oregon from 1975 until his death in 1993. His honorary title of consultant to the Library of Congress, granted to him in 1970, later became the position of poet laureate of the United States.

But this was a quiet and humble man—a conscientious listener as well as a conscientious objector. He chose alternative service during World War II and worked for $2.50 per month in the forests. Many of his poems muse about the consequences of our action or inaction; about the natural world; about relationships with each other and the communities we bump into.

He would get up each morning at four o'clock to work. His daughter, feeling sorry that he was alone, began to get up to keep him company. Then he started getting up at three to write in his journal and to compose—over his lifetime—22,000 poems, a small fraction of which are published in some 57 volumes.

Compassion, humor, wonder at the natural world, and above all, an appreciation for the flawed, imperfect, and beautiful creature the human being is were his subjects, and this simple and profound appreciation of what he observed on earth is his gift to us. Here is one of my favorites, Stafford's "Once in the 40s":

> We were alone one night on a long
> road in Montana. This was in winter, a big
> night, far to the stars. We had hitched,
> my wife and I, and left our ride at
> a crossing to go on. Tired and cold—but
> brave—we trudged along. This, we said

was our life, watched over, allowed to go
where we wanted. We said we'd come back some time
when we got rich. We'd leave the others and find
a night like this, whatever we had to give,
and no matter how far, to be so happy again.

Although he had a PhD from the University of Iowa and taught for over 30 years at Lewis & Clark College in Portland, his writing was always direct, straightforward, and accessible. He was, and is, a great natural treasure—a man who without apology took his seat at life's table under the honorific title of poet.

He wrote a poem for me on a significant occasion in my life. To my knowledge it has never been published, so I share it here as a gift to you.

Saying Goodbye

WILLIAM STAFFORD (1914-1993)
FOR JOHN FROHNMAYER

Is there a good way to do it?
The way bricks do, they lie there on the road
sinking deeper. Some Roman roads—out of sight
now—are waiting in the earth. They become
real again if an earthquake says so,
otherwise they stay disappeared forever.

So is it our duty to witness for what is gone?
It would still be here if we embraced all being
at once, if we held like the arch of a rainbow
too perfect ever to fall. Besides, promises,
they last forever; they always come back:
there is a way to live that holds all that has been.

And—remember—in that real time, nothing is gone.

CHAPTER 6

John Caldwell

Sometimes courage is the quiet voice at the end
of the day saying: "I will try again tomorrow.
—MARY ANNE RADMACHER, writer

Author's note: I asked John Caldwell for his impressions of the slippery and imprecise influence nature and hard physical training have on self-knowledge. Since his book The Cross-Country Ski Book sold over 500,000 copies, I figured he could write. He has been called the "father of Nordic skiing in the United States" and, I suppose, is comparable to that one cow from whom all others are descended. Not only has he coached the best competitors the United States has produced, but his children have raced, coached, and produced their own celebrated racing offspring. Here is his delightful saga.

Jay [Bowerman, see Chapter 17] is nice to say I might have something to say for your project. I am not so sure. I was never much of a racer, never trained scientifically, and sort of fell into a coaching job with the USST [United States Ski Team]. Some background will help explain. It starts out as a bio, but later I have something appropriate.

In 1941 my father took a job as business manager at the Putney [Vermont] School. Putney was founded by Carmelita Hinton, and it surely was one of the earliest co-ed, private boarding schools and very what they now call progressive. Dad's salary included tuition for his kids, four, and so I started as an eighth-grader. I had gone to a local public school in Somerset, Pennsylvania, before the move and was headed for a career in basketball. My father played for Cornell, and he was my coach for a number of years. Despite the fact that I could walk under a fairly tall dining room table without bending my knees, I was the seventh-grade all-star captain of that public school team. Guess I was quick and decently coordinated.

We came to Putney, and the first Christmas vacation—we had five weeks off back then—I walked around the town of Putney with a basketball under my arm, looking for someone to shoot baskets. Putney School didn't have basketball. The kids almost all skied, four days a week. Four days? Yes, we had what Carmelita called the "Out-of-Doors Afternoon Program." This meant that every afternoon, we students were out of doors and either doing work jobs or some kind of sport, with a bit of emphasis on noncompetitive sports. Skiing was the exception here. Carmelita had a daughter, Joan, who was an alternate on the '36 Olympic Alpine team. Her son, Bill, was an accomplished skier, and he gave me one of the best ski lessons I ever had.

So I skied.

The school had a team, and in 1946 we garnered enough gas to compete with other public schools for the state championships. We needed five entries in all four events (cross-country, jumping, downhill, and slalom), and so I volunteered to ski X-C [cross-country] "for the team score." I didn't have any X-C skis and so borrowed my sister's wooden Alpine skis, no edges. I widened the bindings to fit my Alpine boots and galloped around the state championship X-C course. By some miracle we finished second overall and qualified for the New England Championships a week later. I decided I ought to train X-C and so went out in the woods one day, tried to ski fast, quickly got tired, and quit. Going into the New England Championships, I had skied one race and trained one day. I finished 48/52.

I got into Dartmouth and started skiing more seriously and ended up as a good four-event skier by senior year, the 1950 season. In late winter my Nordic coach, "Ja" Densmore, took me to an Eastern Combined meet in Gilford, New Hampshire. The 1950 FIS [International Ski Federation] Nordic Combined Team was there, and I beat a bunch of them. This was enough to encourage me to try out for the 1952 Combined Team to Oslo. I had thought of entering the Alpine tryouts, but they were out West and would have involved a big expenditure of money, which I did not have.

So I entered the tryouts for Nordic, made the team, went to the 1952 Oslo World Games, and got totally beaten. Never before had I been so poorly prepared for any sort of competition, including Tiddly-Winks. I was already coaching the year after college, and this trip to Oslo was a defining moment. Simply put, I wanted to make sure no US skiers ever went to another Games so poorly prepared.

That started my coaching career, more seriously than the year before.

I mogged along, went to various Eastern Ski Association meetings, had a few good X-C skiers out of Putney (where

I was coaching), and slowly moved up to what one might call a position of prominence in the X-C world during the '50s and early '60s.

During this time I was training juniors and some seniors at divisional training camps and all the while trying to figure out the best way to train Americans, where X-C was kind of a lost sport. I was heavily influenced by my Putney upbringing, the out-of-doors stuff and camping trips (two to three every year), and physical activity. I looked for something which I thought might help keep skiers engaged in the sport for many years, something they could adapt as a lifestyle. As I monkeyed around, I realized that it's really a privilege to take a walk, or a run, or a ski, or whatever, in the out-of-doors in Vermont.

When I eventually became the US Team's X-C coach, I continued to train the skiers using unusual approaches. We had no money to speak of in the budget for training camps. I was never paid until 1972, and so it was a stretch to manage training camps for the skiers. But my sister worked at the Waterville Valley ski area [in Vermont], and she arranged for room and board for our skiers in return for some work, like cutting brush, stacking wood, and so on. That was a deal for an inexpensive training camp. The skiers only had to get to Waterville Valley. One year we had both the men's and women's teams there, and I scheduled a trip to the Tri-Pyramids and back for our workout. Perfect! The guys got out into the wilderness, had a good hike, saw some great views, and everything was fine. The women meanwhile did intervals around the road loop in the valley, where they got good views of all the inns and gas stations. Afterwards, they were pissed. So I knew I was onto something.

In 1968, for our national training camp, I scheduled a hike of the Long Trail in Vermont, about 270 miles in nine days. There was incentive provided—you make the day's hike, and you get a bunk and dinner. Bad weather? Our reservations are for tonight. You can't make it? See ya later. A number of the skiers told me that was the best training they had ever done—averaging thirty miles a day, blisters and sore muscles notwithstanding.

That was good. So the next year I scheduled an 800-mile bike trip around New England. Back then it was considered quite an accomplishment to do one hundred miles in a day. So we started in the Cambridge, Massachusetts, area on a very rainy day (don't forget our reservations); and after a couple of days, as the bikers learned to ride and draft, the workouts were too easy, so on a couple of occasions I had to add some short running intervals at the end of the bike tour.

I guess I was trying to instill camaraderie and adventure in the team. We didn't have any real studs, no equipment manufacturers loading us with equipment, etc. So it's notable to mention that at the 1980 Olympics in Lake Placid, the US relay team—four racers—all belonged to the Putney Ski Club—Tim Caldwell, Stan Dunklee, Bill Koch, and Jim Galanes. The Putney Ski Club boasted thirty-seven members, dues a buck a year. These guys trained together, pushed each other, all without a formal coach, all without any money for endorsements, but just for the love of the sport (and clearly for the good feelings after workouts, which Jay [Bowerman] and Jon [Chaffee, see Chapter 27] have described).

This group (with the addition of Dan Simoneau—another Easterner) went on to become one of the best men's teams in the world during the 1982 season. In sheer ranking and results, this team's record has not been approached since.

I think my training methods instilled a tradition and are still used today. I always had this idea of having a goal in training, either daily or for a longer time (thus the Long Trail hike). Workouts were often done as a point-to-point maneuver rather than doing loops, for instance.

X-C is not a big sport in the US. Our X-C heroes are not guaranteed jobs after they retire from the sport. A small percentage of sports fans have even heard of them, and this situation continues to the present time. As I write this, our men's program is in dire straits. Skiers are turning down offered trips to Europe and are asking themselves what's in it for me? There have to be some kind of rewards for giving up several years to train up to a level where you are not embarrassed to race in Europe. Maybe we'd be wise to go back to the "olden days."

Well, I trained hard enough a few times to "run out of groceries," but that was many years ago. Except two days ago I ran out for the first time in years, after doing nothing to warrant it. When this happens, all I think about is grabbing the peanut butter jar, some bread and mayonnaise, and a home brew to wash the energy-providing food down. It worked the other day just as well as it used to work.

I'm 91 and not able to exercise much. My chief exercise is walking with ski poles, and since I live on a sidehill, a vast majority of my walks start on an uphill. I have always been a nut on technique, and so with walking I try to use appropriate leg muscles as well as with my ski pole efforts. It's easy for me to sense strain in my back, for instance, and if that occurs, I change my technique. I listen to my heart and know when I have approached anaerobic threshold and keep my pace with that in mind. I don't use a PR [heartrate monitor] anymore, but I used to row a lot and knew my threshold was right around 142. Now, no doubt, it is lower, but that is not a concern.

When the walking gets in sync with my efforts and I don't need to think about technique, I get into a groove, usually an idea groove, and come up with my best ideas for the day. I make plans after the walk.

It's all pretty simple, and quite enjoyable.

CHAPTER 7

Practically Born to the Sport

Not yesterday I learned to know / The love of bare November days…

—ROBERT FROST, poet

Ryan Gage was on skis by the age of two. He grew up in Government Camp, a small mountain town at the base of the road leading up to Timberline Lodge on Mount Hood. He has raced, coached, and worked in the industry all his life. Work for pay started at age nine, so he could afford to buy a ski pass. He has worked at Mount Bachelor for the last twenty years in snowcat operations, snow removal, racing, lift maintenance, facilities maintenance, building and removing chairs, and installing snow-making equipment. His title is director of base operations.

I hit him with the "Have you ever had a mystical experience on the mountain?" question and get the blank stare that such a bell-bottomed-guru question deserves. But then he starts to talk about the peaceful times he has had in a snowcat when he is the only person on the mountain and probably the only one awake within a fifteen-mile perimeter. "You have to be there," he says. "That is time that is just mine. It is total peace just roaming around the mountain in my cat."

In a heavy snow cycle, when you're pushing the snow with 7,000 pounds of hydraulic force, you can't go more than ten feet sometimes before you have to back up and do it again. "We have clocked 170 mile per hour winds here," Ryan says. "When the snow is swirling, sometimes the best you can do is turn off the lights and try to see the shadows. During weather events your surroundings are always becoming; and no matter how well you know the mountain, the cornice formations can change and sweep you and your machine away. When you are in that slide, with your heart in your mouth, it is like driving through a snow blower. Pure vertigo."

We agree that that is not a mystical experience.

"We have eighteen snowcat operators, and there is a great camaraderie among us. We know the drivers on the other mountains around here, and many of these guys and gals see each other in the summers working construction, fighting wildfires, river guiding. Some do golf course maintenance, and some have farms." These are people who are wedded to the out-of-doors.

"Has there been an experience that changed your attitude toward snow grooming?" I wondered. Here is what he told me:

I was asked to join the team that built the courses for the 2015 FIS World Alpine Ski Championships at Beaver Creek, Colorado. The run I was preparing was named "The Abyss." It had about a forty-degree slope, so the Beaver Creek supervisor told me to tie off my winch to a tree at the top, which I did. I had only a couple of more passes to complete over the slick, man-made snow. The slope angled toward a ravine with a creek at the bottom.

Out of the corner of my eye I see this object coming at me which is the tree, accelerating with both the lack of winch resistance and gravity. It smashes into my windshield, pivots around and hits the door, and I am sliding down the Abyss wondering how deep the creek is. Since I am going backwards, I can't use the blade to try to slow down, and at four in the morning I am literally headed for shit creek. After a lifetime, I stop about one hundred feet from the creek. I get on the radio, and two other operators are there to help me in a jiffy.

That changed me as an operator. It was a bad night. But I got back in the saddle and kept on grooming. Well, not in that machine. Turns out it was a demo, and the manufacturer fixed it, Mt. Bachelor [ski resort] bought it, and it is still in service. It wasn't the machine's fault that the tree decided to travel.

Working night shift alone in the cab of a PistenBully isn't for everyone, but you see some of the most amazing sunrises and sunsets. At night out there, you are not part of the rest of the world. Every shift is different. Nature has an inexhaustible repertoire. I suppose that is mystical in and of itself.

CHAPTER 8

Communications

The weather is here; wish you were beautiful.

—POSTCARD INSCRIPTION

Some mountains have cell phone service, which has made the sport safer and also led to lots of phones being dropped off the lift from cold, fumbling fingers. Good luck with finding that. Then there are the two-way radios used by the ski patrol, mountain hosts and grooming operators. And finally there are the two-way radios for keeping track of your kids. Here is a real conversation, and as humor columnist Dave Barry would say, I am not making this up:

Mom: Where are you? Over.

Kid: I am in the bathroom. Over.

Mom: Where? Over.

Kid: In the lodge. And Mom, I didn't pee in my boot this time. Over.

Mom: That's good. Be sure and wash your hands. Over.

Kid: O.K. Over.

Is this a great country or what?

In Montana if you slide off the road the police will come along and give you a ticket for failing to maintain control. Chum and Sally have one of the most beautiful pieces of property on this earth. It sits against the front range of the Bridger Mountains looking west over the Gallatin Valley and features trout-stocked ponds, a rushing creek, and shaggy, golden-coated Scottish Highland cattle. Chum had just left his driveway on his way to town when his four-wheel-drive rig slid off the road. A cop arrived, got out of her patrol car and walked to where Chum was standing by his ditched vehicle. Meanwhile, her driverless car started sliding all by itself. As she turned to watch, she started to slip, and Chum grabbed her arm to keep her from falling. "I would feel pretty silly giving you a ticket," she said, and, gingerly, retreated to her car to call for two tow trucks. Winter will have its way with you. It demands and deserves respect. It is awesome and breathtaking.

The word spiritual derives from the Latin word for breathing—an activity crucial to life itself. I think the shortness of breath (a different kind of breathtaking) we flatlanders experience on the mountain is part of what makes the experience so special. The atmosphere is telling us that things are different here; life is harder here. You have to earn your activity in a more rigorous way.

Paying attention to breathing is a big part of yoga and many spiritual exercises, and it is a very big part of singing. Michael Gesme, the gifted conductor of the Central Oregon

Symphony is the only orchestral conductor I have sung with who breathes with the chorus while conducting. The orchestra will be playing along, and his cue for the chorus entry will be a big, deep breath. It really helps.

Singing together is mystical—spiritual, at least. Every five years in Estonia, thirty thousand singers and another hundred thousand citizens and visitors gather to sing patriotic songs together. It is not just a remembrance of a history filled with invasions and barbarity; it is a reaffirmation of the dignity and community that they share. Similarly, the fourth movement of Beethoven's Ninth Symphony is the Ode to Joy, in which all men are declared to be brothers. With all of his genius, Beethoven felt that the human voice, the human breath, was necessary to reach the sublime.

Here is just one more example that literally took our breath away. As I write this, it happened last night, February 13, 2020, at the Hult Center for the Performing Arts in Eugene, Oregon. Maestro Jeffrey Kahane had just played Beethoven's Fourth Piano Concerto, brilliantly, conducting from the keyboard. The audience wouldn't let him go, so he sat back down and began to play. Softly. What tune is this? Then we realized it was America the Beautiful, in a lyrical, flowing and moving orchestration. Then he abruptly shifted to a minor, discordant, strident bashing of the bass keys. Slowly the melody reappeared and wandered in no recognizable style or progression. Then it was over, but he kept his hands depressed on the keys. We, the audience, sat there. Stunned. What did we just hear? Dare we applaud?

The music spoke to our dismay, and the love that we feel for this country. A letter to the local newspaper put it this way: "Unexpected tears streamed down my cheeks with despair for what has become of our country. An electorate so polarized and divided and unwilling to listen, learn and work together. Vindictive, uncivil discourse, disinformation and lack of ethics and morals at the highest levels…. I didn't realize how deeply I felt until I was moved by the music…"

Later an usher told me that an orchestra member who could see Maestro Kahane's face (his back was to the audience as he sat at the keyboard) said he, too, had tears in his eyes. It appeared that he had improvised it, and it was profoundly mystical.

CHAPTER 9

Dangers

There is nothing wrong with fear; the only mistake is
to let it stop you in your tracks.

—TWYLA THARP, choreographer

The mountain can kill you. Some of the dangers look
pretty obvious, like skiing below a cornice or jumping
off a cliff onto the rocks. But some appear benign, like tree
wells—the deadliest killer of all. You ski or ride too close to
the tree and the snow gives way, leaving you hanging upside
down, still in your bindings. Every time you struggle you
dislodge more snow into your face until you can't breathe,
and then you are done. It is a nasty way to go.

Saplings are another trap. They just look lumpy under
new snow, but they can grab your skis and hold you down just
like snags beneath the surface in a river, and you can't breathe
or move enough to save yourself. Then there is skiing into a
tree. Avoid this. In Sun Valley, they call it a birch tree implant.
Farther west it is the unforgiving bark of a hemlock, as bad
for the body as the liquid Socrates drank—a heartless killer.

Few ski into the trees on purpose. It is usually occurs
in a whiteout, when a skier is going too fast with too little

visibility, or as the result of a fall. Several years ago I was skiing too fast along the edge of a run when a skier in front of me made an unexpected turn (my fault; she had the right-of-way), and I caught an edge. As I was flying through the air, I wrenched my right shoulder in a throwing motion, landed face first and went sliding toward the trees. Broken neck at best, I thought, as the world slowed down for the disaster. I stopped short of the trees, and the shoulder was the only casualty—but I could have been dead. I tell this as a cautionary tale to myself and others. Skiing is a dangerous sport; and stupid skiing is, well, stupid. Einstein said, "The difference between stupidity and genius is that genius has its limits." There is, unfortunately, plenty of stupid to go around.

An avalanche can happen to anyone, even the most experienced skiers. Oz, who for years ran the snowcat skiing at Mount Bailey by Diamond Lake in Southern Oregon, was caught in one that carried him into the trees. Even with a locating beacon, which backcountry skiers carry, you need someone to find you and dig you out. It doesn't take long for the snow to harden like cement.

My brother Phil and I were skiing years ago at Mount Ashland, also in Southern Oregon, when the lift failed late in the afternoon. The patrol took the skiers down chair by chair by throwing a rope over the cable and then repelling each skier down on a T-bar. By the time they got to us, it was dark, and I mean December dark. I do not recommend skiing in the dark.

Part of the ethos of the mountain is taking care of each other. Skiers warn of dangers, take care of injuries, yell at reckless and dangerous activity. Every year, though, people get hurt. The wives of two of my ski friends suffered broken bones from separate collisions that were not their fault.

One of the great tragedies touching near to me involved the deaths of seven students and two teachers from Portland's Oregon Episcopal School in 1986. The program in which they were involved, called Basecamp, was designed to test and stretch individually imposed limitations climaxing with an ascent of 11,247-foot Mount Hood. They got caught in a storm, and only two survived. These were the best and the brightest, friends of my kids, and the parents were friends and colleagues as well. I remember looking out at the mountain as the search parties and helicopters were trying to find their hastily constructed snow cave and thinking that it wasn't the mountain's fault; it was a failure to respect the mountain and the unpredictable power of nature.

In that same winter three young people on our street of maybe twenty houses died on the mountain: one with the Oregon Episcopal School, one who skied into a tree, and one a patroller who thought the charge he was holding wasn't lit. "Acceptable losses?" Absolutely not.

Terry Blaylock, the retail manager of Gravity Sports at Mt. Bachelor resort who has worked in the industry for fifty years, talks of a rescue effort triggered by a twelve-year-old boy who was alone in the parking lot. He said his dad had intended to ski the summit and had not returned. It was getting dark, and the ski patrol rounded up volunteers like an old-time posse. Terry and others snowmobiled up to the lift shack, fired up the summit chair, and started off in twos looking for tracks. A couple of patrollers reported by radio that they had found tracks crossing the catch line. They followed and saw where the skier hesitated—a place already a quarter mile below the get-back. The patrollers followed the tracks and found the skier. What made it all worthwhile was the radio exchange between the boy and his father:

"I love you dad. I'm glad you're safe."

A man said to the universe

STEPHEN CRANE (1871-1900)

A man said to the universe:
"Sir, I exist!"
"However," replied the universe,
"The fact has not created in me
a sense of obligation."

CHAPTER 10

Woofers

The greater the difficulty, the more glory in surmounting it.

—EPICURUS, Greek philosopher

No, a woofer is not some kind of exotic dog trainer. Woofer, or WFR, stands for wilderness first responder. These people are trained in basic life support, treatment of physical trauma, fractures, sprains, spinal injuries, dislocations, and onset of sudden illnesses that happen in remote locations. Their extensive training (usually about eighty hours' worth) is on top of whatever CPR, emergency medical technician, or other medical certifications they already have.

Annie McCormack is a woofer working out of Mt. Bachelor's Nordic Center. She covers over fifty kilometers of regularly groomed trails plus the large oval for skate skiers, the dogsled route and then, if skiers choose to break their own trails, wherever they might be for miles around in the Deschutes National Forest.

What could happen? You could fall and break a leg; a tree could fall on you; you could become lost or disoriented;

or you could feel faint, short of breath, or light-headed. Just about any malady that could befall you in town could happen miles from definitive medical care. Annie's job is first to find you, then to evaluate, stabilize, and evacuate you to a suitable facility.

While Nordic skiing is not as fast as downhill, the hazards are unmarked, the terrain can be tricky and, for many who are used to the stability of downhill skis, the Nordic boards can be frustratingly uncontrollable. An accident miles from the lodge, particularly late on a winter afternoon, can be positively scary.

Annie has boarded and downhilled, but to her, Nordic feels more natural—like a primitive hunter going out into the woods, finding some prey, and dragging it back to camp. When you are way out there, you are really alone. You can see all around you, and your limbic brain is quiet because nothing is chasing you. There is a sense of peace—no sabertoothed tigers or grizzlies are lurking there ready to have you for lunch. You become one with nature.

In Nordic skiing, you make a decision based on four yards ahead, rather than a hundred yards as in downhill. While the adrenaline may be less, the aerobic body is working hard, and the mind has time to wander and to take in the surroundings and marvel at what nature's winter has to offer.

There are white-gowned hemlocks and layers of blue-black clouds carrying the impending storm. Strips of sunlight and shadow illuminate, define and conceal. When it starts softly to snow, the world is quiet, the forest serene.

A Nordic skier who is also a photographer was out taking pictures, and everything was black and white—and then along came the ski team, all in bright red uniforms.

Then came the dogs, pulling and barking with the sled passengers bundled under a tarp. Then the forest was silent again, unperturbed, inert, but at the same time quivering with life.

Some of the most rewarding outings—at least for the camp robbers—are the full moon, clear sky midnight treks to the warming hut at the Virginia Meissner Nordic Area southwest of Bend. All you have to do is stand there with a PowerBar in your outstretched hand, and they will fly down, take it in their beak and, without a nod or a thank-you, flitter off. They probably eat better in winter than summer.

Where It Is Winter

GEORGE O'NEIL (1896-1940)

Now there is frost upon the hill
And no leaf stirring in the wood;
The little streams are cold and still;
Never so still has winter stood.
Never so held as in this hollow,
Beneath these hemlocks dark and low,
Brooding this hour that hours must follow
Burdened with snow. . . .
Now there is nothing, no confusion,
To shield against the silence here;
And spirits, barren of illusions,
To whom all agonies are clear,
Rush on the naked heart and cry
Of every poignant shining thing
Where there is little left to die
And no more Spring.

CHAPTER 11

Mysticism

One's action ought to come out of an achieved
stillness: not to be a mere rushing on.

—D.H. LAWRENCE, writer

M ysticism may invoke the image of a guru sitting cross-
legged on a mountaintop, or the fact-free, airy-fairy
fantasy of the hopelessly out of touch. It is, however, a vener-
able religious tradition in both East and West, and it is worth
a serious look, even if words will fail us in its description.

William James, in his seminal book The Varieties of
Religious Experience (1902) suggests four characteristics
that describe mysticism. The first is what he calls inef-
fability, namely that it cannot be described and therefore
must be experienced. It is more a state of feeling than
of intellect. The second is a noetic quality, meaning that
those who experience it have studied, prepared, and made
themselves receptive. The third is transiency—it doesn't last
long, cannot be reproduced, and is remembered imperfectly.
Fourth is passivity; that is, the recipient cannot call the
experience into being even though rehearsal and preparation may invite it. It comes and goes of its own will.

James suggests that music and lyric poetry fetch "vague vistas of a life continuous with our own, beckoning and inviting, yet ever eluding our pursuit." It is the common feeling of déjà vu (or as Yogi Berra would say, "déjà vu all over again")—the feeling that we have been here before. James quotes Tennyson's "The Two Voices":

> *Moreover, something is or seems,*
> *That touches me with mystic gleams,*
> *Like glimpses of forgotten dreams—*
> *Of something felt, like something here;*
> *Of something done, I know not where;*
> *Such as no language may declare.*

Nature can awaken mystical moods, and James reported that most occurrences he collected in his psychological studies happened out-of-doors. Sunsets, mountains, oceans, and butterflies are often windows to the mystical. Mountaineers summiting Oregon's South Sister report swarms of tortoise-shell butterflies up there dancing around and making whoopee in the rarified air. Real ones, but mystical all the same. One hiker was heard to say: "We are trying to give them some privacy but…"

Yoga, with its emphasis on passivity, breathing, intellectual and moral discipline, and body control is an age-old avenue into what is not visible or reachable in our world. Christian, Jewish, Buddhist, Hindu, Islamic, and Native American religions, along with scores of other sects and faiths, have found ways to communicate with spirits and forces outside our world. It is fair to say, as well, that this has been fertile ground for charlatans and hucksters throughout the ages.

One thing is sure: our time on the mountain is directed by the cosmic curtain puller. The clouds roll in and disappear without pattern or decodable intent. The vistas that are clear become obscure; the vivid, swirling, confusing, and elating movements are not of our making. While all of us may experience these differently, there is, I believe, a universal sense triggered by nature that we are but a small, insignificant part of a universe both seen and unseen.

Is it mystical to make a track down the uncut snow? Is it painting the cosmic canvas as we look back at our tracks? Does the rhythm of the turns and the floating through the powder link up with some vibration from deep in the mountain that we have no ability to define, but nonetheless can intuit?

Self-contradiction seems to be part of the way imperfect language describes the indescribable: dazzling obscurity, whispering silence, silent music, thundering calm. And yet, if you ask an experienced skier if he or she has ever had a mystical experience, the answer is likely to be: "Everyday." When I asked that question of one skier on the chair, she responded: "I have only been skiing for five days. Maybe on day six."

There's a certain Slant of light

EMILY DICKINSON (1830-1886)

There's a certain Slant of light.
Winter Afternoons—
That oppresses, like the Heft
Of Cathedral Tunes—

Heavenly Hurt, it gives us—
We can find no scar,
But internal difference,
Where the Meanings are—

None may teach it—Any—
'Tis the seal Despair—
An imperial affliction
Sent us of the Air—

When it comes, the Landscape listens—
Shadows—hold their breath—
When it goes, 'tis like the Distance
On the look of Death—

CHAPTER 12

Into the Teeth
of Winter

If we are not laughed at, it would not be
sufficient to be Tao.

—TAO TE CHING

A television program entitled Yellowstone in Winter was
what started it. The park looked so magical, so primal,
so earthy. There were bison shaking their shaggy heads to
clear away the snow and expose the grass; there were geysers
throwing water hundreds of feet into the air; the skies were
blue, the snow pristine. What could be better? And we had
a four-wheel-drive car, finally, after years of messing with
tire chains. We were good to go.

The car was an impossibly small Toyota Tercel wagon,
a new model in 1983. As it turned out, the car's back end
had a tendency to want to pass the front, but I get ahead of
myself. We put four pairs of skis on the rack, crammed all
of our boots and bags into the back until it simply wouldn't
hold any more, and took off from Portland in a snowstorm
on a 2,200-mile odyssey—my wife, Leah; sons Jason, age

twelve-and-a-half, and Aaron, age eleven; and me, a city lawyer totally unequipped to take on nature. First stop was Idaho Falls to pick up a snowmobile from the brother of our Portland friend whose father had a remote cabin near Driggs, Idaho, which, in turn, was near the Grand Targhee ski area, our first destination. We were just ahead of a major storm—in fact, they were closing the roads behind us—but we didn't know any better because the snow we were used to came down in wet blobs, and this snow was fine and swirly. God help the clueless.

After a five-minute rehearsal on how to run a snowmobile, we hitched up the trailer, which was about as big as the car, and took off for Driggs. The road to the cabin was near three big Harvestore silos where there was a ranch house. The road itself was indistinguishable under the snow. So Leah and the boys holed up with the farm family, while I—the intrepid explorer—mounted the snow machine and took off to blaze trail to the cabin. I got about one hundred yards, and the machine sank. So, I hopped off in snow up to my crotch, horsed it around, drove back on my track, horsed it around again, and roared on for another hundred yards, and then repeated the process again and again. After doing this for about an hour, it occurred to me that—sweating profusely, with still no cabin in sight—I could freeze to death out here. Instead, I found the cabin and headed back to pick up the troops. As I approached the farmhouse, through the blowing snow, there was Aaron, in ski boots and goggles, bouncing on an outdoor trampoline.

We got to the cabin, turned on the lights, turned on the water…turned on the water…turned on the water. Pipes were frozen. What to eat? We hadn't shopped because there was no room in the car for groceries. Saltines and tea were all we could find. Meanwhile, the snow was coming down nonstop—like twenty-four inches that night. So the next day we dug out the car, skied at Targhee and had a fine time, except that Jason was feeling sick and it was still snowing and a bunch of the roads were closed. At least we now had food, and we had tied rags and sponges around the offending pipes, and water was mostly going through them. Over our days there, Leah got to be on a first-name basis with the road report lady at the state police.

Jason was still feeling bum so we decided that Aaron and I would go over the pass to ski at Jackson Hole the next day. Leah drove down to the car on the snowmobile with me and returned to the cabin to fetch Aaron. I was cleaning off the car when I saw them coming down the hill, Aaron driving with Leah on the back. "Going nice and slow like a responsible kid," I thought. Then, about twenty yards from the car, he gunned it, Leah bailed off the back before the impending disaster, and Aaron crashed the snowmobile into the car. He rolled around holding his leg or I would have killed him on the spot. Both vehicles were drivable, so Aaron and I headed to the emergency room at Driggs. The Doc looked him over, pronounced him damage-free, and Aaron hopped off the examining table (he later confessed that he was never hurt, but needed a diversion; he was trying to pull a brodie like he had seen the sheriff do on his snow machine when two deputies had come by to check on us the day before, but at about 80 pounds he was 150 pounds too light and twenty years too green).

We proceeded on to Jackson to ski. Even at that age, Aaron was a better skier than I, and I told him not to take off and leave me since neither of us knew the area. He did exactly that, so I pulled his ticket, and we returned to the cabin. What a great day.

The rest of the journey is a blur. I remember a trip through Yellowstone in a snow coach and sliding into a ditch and having to get pulled out (actually a major axle jerk out) by an accommodating farmer. Between Driggs and Jackson Hole we had to stop for a herd of pink pigs in the road. (It is properly called "a sounder of swine" although somehow I can't imagine those words coming out of my mouth: "Oh look, dear, it's a sounder of swine.")

I remember the mystical experience of a clearing sky after the multiday storm with the refreshed monochromatic landscape. It was a renewal like God's rainbow promise to Noah.

We trekked on to Schweitzer, got in plenty of turns, and returned to Oregon, where the landscape looked riotously colorful after so many days of black and white. Would I do it again? Naw, once was enough. But like disasters that fade into mishaps, the memories are fond.

Oh, and about that car; we kept it long enough that every one of us—that is Leah, Jason, Aaron, and I—did at least one unplanned 360-degree slide. I did a terrifying 720. Nobody got killed, thank goodness, but the back end was definitely in a bigger hurry than the front.

CHAPTER 13

Timberline Lodge

The best history has to give us is the enthusiasm
which it arouses.

—GOETHE, poet and writer

I f you want inspiration on the mountain; if you want to be
mystically transported back to the late 1930s; if you want
to see how man can build with what nature provides, spend
a day at Timberline Lodge. It sits, not surprisingly, at the
timberline on Mount Hood, with the brilliant, snow-covered
summit of the mountain dominating views from the back,
and vistas of Mount Jefferson and other Cascade Peaks from
the front. The ski area is both above the lodge and down in the
trees below and is mostly gentle (no "take your breath away"
steeps), but plenty of fun. The Phlox Point Hut, which used
to be a Boy Scout shelter, has a circle of Adirondack chairs
around a fire pit for the hearty to catch some sun, or stars,
and with the exception of the Wy'East Day Lodge, built in
1981 to take pressure off the main lodge, which was getting
kicked to death by ski boots, the whole area has the feel of
a simpler time—closer to the earth and to the elements. A
million people a year come to see this monument that dem-

onstrates that something grand, reassuring, and life-affirming can emerge from economic disaster.

The Forest Service had plans to build a ski/hiking lodge on Mount Hood from about 1924. There were a few primitive structures where the hearty could stay overnight if they brought their own blanket, but skiing was in its infancy. Then along came the Great Depression, and people were struggling just to survive. President Franklin D. Roosevelt's policy was to try programs to see if they worked, and the Works Progress Administration (WPA) along with the Civilian Conservation Corps (CCC) and various arts projects were put into place to give people jobs, and not incidentally, to create improvements such as roads, dams, and this magnificent structure.

Construction got underway in 1936 after workers built a road to the site and cleared snow eighteen feet deep. Over five hundred men and women worked on the project, many of them over the age of fifty-five. It was completed, ahead of schedule, in eighteen months and dedicated on September 28, 1937, by FDR himself (just the week before his visit, workers built a special chair with arms so the president could lift himself up to speak).

The original plan has two wings, set apart at a 120-degree angle, with a hexagonal "head house" meant to mimic the shape of the mountain joining the two. The head house has a massive fireplace and support tower made from stones gathered on the mountain. The huge, square beams that emerge like wagon wheel spokes from the fireplace tower are of ponderosa pine logs from the Columbia National Forest (now the Gifford Pinchot National Forest) in Washington.

Entry in the winter is protected by a metal awning shed that catches the snow as it slides off the steep roof. You immediately know you are in a different world. On your left is a glass mosaic of a bear catching a fish, a deer looking alert, and the mountain flowers, trees, and critters. The focal point is the multisided fireplace in the center with handcrafted chairs and benches suitable for skiers to relax and regroup. It even has drain channels in the floor for melting snow.

Also in the lower level is the Rachael Griffin Historic Exhibition Center, displaying a model of an original guestroom and the rude implements with which the craftspeople loomed, chiseled, chopped, and stitched. It has rugs that were hooked out of remnants of old CCC uniforms, metal andirons forged from scrap, and crosscut saws, broad axes, and adzes used to form the beams. Everywhere one turns in the lodge are examples of craftsmanship and ingenuity. For example, newel posts on the stairways have carved animals on top. These cedar posts started their lives outside the forest as power poles.

Workers were paid ninety cents per hour and sometimes in the winter had to hold on to a rope stretched from their transport truck to the lodge door when the blizzard made navigation impossible. Yet the construction went without incident or mishap. Furniture and soft fabrics (over seven hundred yards of woven material) were produced in warehouses, school basements—anywhere space could be found in Portland. Few of the masons or carpenters were experts. Those on the job who had skills taught the others. The best blacksmith was said to be a man in a wheelchair who had massive arms. The expert

German watercolor artist was rescued from living in an old piano box and eating cold noodles.

On the main level, the center fireplaces again dominate, but all around the structure are nooks and seating arrangements that lend themselves to conversation, reading, drinking hot chocolate, or just sitting there admiring this magnificent structure made of stone buttresses, logs and boards, iron fittings, and creative genius. Same is true with the surrounding mezzanine, again with nooks for quiet conversation, the Ram's Head bar for libations, and views of Mount Jefferson to the south and the majestic peak of Mount Hood sloping up from the back windows.

The test of fine art is time. The works of C.S. Price, Charles Heaney, the Runquist brothers, Douglas Lynch, and many others pass that test beautifully, not just because they capture the spirit and everyday lives of the people who built the lodge and struggled through the Great Depression, but because they speak to us today about our own struggles, our own uncertainties, and our own reverence for nature. The art is not incidental or decorative; it is fundamental to all that the lodge is and aspires to be. It represents the spirit of the people, and the spirit of the mountain. It is the mystical representation of the hunger of humankind for beauty. Thomas Jefferson thought architecture and democracy were handmaidens since in a democracy, public buildings are for the people. FDR agreed, and said in his inaugural remarks that the lodge gave to the people a place to play in all seasons of the year.

Timberline closed during World War II and by 1954 was in a state of disrepair. Dick Kohnstamm and his wife, Molly, operated the lodge from 1955 on and saved it. They treated it as if it were their own and went into debt spending their own money to maintain it. But skiing boomed in the 1960s, and Timberline was the hot place to be cold. Christmas reservations there were drooled over in the pages of Playboy magazine—and remain objects of desire to this day, with winter holiday accommodations booked more than a year in advance.

By the time of his death in 2006, Dick had lovingly tended to the lodge for over fifty years. A pair of St. Bernard dogs were always on hand to help. Today, his family corporation still runs the lodge, and he is a hero of the first order, having shepherded Timberline through the Forest Service's construction of a new wing in 1975 and multiple restoration and enhancement projects undertaken by Friends of Timberline—all designed to preserve its magic. Treat yourself to a visit.

CHAPTER 14

Joe Leonard

The greatest gift given me is my
ability to take risks.

—JOE LEONARD

J oe Leonard's formal schooling never saw a high school
graduation, but his life has been one of constant self-
education. He quotes Goethe: "The moment one definitely
commits oneself, providence moves, too….Boldness has
genius, power and magic in it." He spent his first five years
in the shadow of the Sawtooth Mountains in Idaho, and
they have never left him.

I had heard about him—he is something of a legend—
and I talked to him on the telephone before I read his exqui-
sitely titled book, "The Son of the Madam of the Mustang
Ranch." Buy it and savor it; it has many more lessons about
taking life by the scruff of the neck and going after it than
I can recount here. But it is true—his mother did run the
infamous Nevada brothel. At one point, Joe worked there
as a security guard, and a guy was pointing a gun at him
out a pickup window when Joe's German shepherd, Duke,
saved him by clamping his jaws around the guy's arm. All

in a day's work. Not the right kind of work, though. One of the girls in the bordello asked Joe if he knew God. He demurred, and she gave him Edgar Cayce's small book "There is a River," which he read that day and credits with changing his life. He quit his job, dropped his pistol into the river and turned toward photography, mountains, and whitewater kayaking. He and his partner John Zapp made the first winter ascents of peaks in Idaho's Sawtooth Range and White Cloud Mountains, and he filled his life with dimensions most of us would describe as heroic.

He is a great storyteller and if what appears here differs from his book, well, that is what stories are supposed to do—get richer with the flow of the conversation. But blame any unintentional inaccuracies on my notetaking and translation.

Joe was an inexperienced climber but wanted to climb 14,179-foot Mount Shasta in Northern California on New Year's Day, 1966. The group of four included two experienced Sierra Club climbers who left the midway tent early to summit the mountain. The wind was howling nearly one hundred miles per hour. Joe and his partner Jim Backus were about an hour behind and took a route up a couloir, where they had to hack steps in the ice. It was not steep enough to rope up, but hacking steps was hard work, and they spelled each other as they went. Joe turned to take a photo, looked back, and Backus was nowhere to be seen. He was just gone. Stories the night before about Martians in caves popping up and having climbers for lunch filled his mind.

He could see down the mountain. Backus hadn't fallen. What to do? He had to find out, so he climbed, and fell—not down, but up. The wind was sailing him skyward at a ferocious pace. It swept him over the lip, and he grabbed a rock pinnacle but couldn't hold on, went flying over the edge and landed—plop—in soft snow right next to his partner. "What took you so long, Joe?" Had they landed anywhere but that small patch of soft snow, they would have been dead and dead. They decided that was enough excitement for one day, and the summit could wait.

The call of the Sawtooth Mountains was irresistible, and Joe and friend John Zapp decided they would be the first to climb Mount Regan in winter. They failed twice in the late 1960s, and again a third time in an assault of Castle Peak in Idaho's White Cloud Mountains. They succeeded in gaining the summit of Mount Regan on the fourth try. In one misadventure, they encountered rain, got totally soaked, and were close to freezing to death, having abandoned their ice-soaked gear in an attempt to make it back to civilization. Exhausted and plodding one ski through the ice crust after the other, almost in a trance, Joe heard a female voice say: "He watches over the lost and wandering." He writes, "That moment in the wilds of the Sawtooth Mountains strikes me still as the greatest blessing of my life."

Another time, coming out of the wilderness, tired and needing a cup of coffee in the town of Clayton, Joe and John saw all sorts of cars around but no people. The lady in the post office suggested they go across the street, so they went down some stairs, opened the door, and a room full of people turned, stopped talking, and stared at these two longhaired, knicker-clad young men. This was 1967. Coffee wasn't on the menu, so they made their way to the bar, ordered a beer and a whiskey, and turned around. The crowd, mostly men but a few women, and tough-looking miners all, were still staring. A little guy came out of a side door followed by a few others—right up close—and stuck his nose in Joe's face and said: "What are you: hippies, queers, or mountaineers?" Joe thought, "What is worst?" So he said, "Mountaineers," and suddenly everybody was excited and wanted to know all about it.

In those days, nobody went into the wilderness in the winter.

For Joe, it was opportunity. He knew the popularity of wilderness ski touring in Europe, and after they acquired Norge ski equipment from Scandinavia, a brand that was light, sturdy and inexpensive, they were in business as the first backcountry Alpine guides in the United States. Whitewater kayaking followed with whitewater rodeos (as dangerous as those on land but without bulls), and ski yurts for ski touring. He tells of one avalanche that didn't kill them, multiple close calls with death on the water, and a life guided by his own spiritual quest.

Here are his own words: "Throughout my life I have constantly been confronted by mountains, some unyielding and unforgiving, some which have been beyond recognition and understanding, and many that seemed unconquerable, but all have been of my own creation…In my mountains I have found my light shining through the darkness."

"My excursions into the mystical; hearing voices, experiencing the power of prayer, or for just an instant experiencing separation of mind and body…have been gifts…I have found my home in nature."

CHAPTER 15

Jewish Mysticism

The belt of the wise is burst by this
mysterious cause of causes."

—KABBALAH

S ome forms of religious mysticism connect directly
with sport such as the Hindu yogins who, according
to legend, could reduce their heart rate, lower their body
temperature, and modify their breathing, all by force of
will. The quest for achieving the highest bodily potential is
at the heart of all competitive sport, and the finest athletes
can do things with their bodies that are the stuff of dreams
for us mere mortals.

Jewish mysticism is a centuries-old tradition seeking,
in part, to transcend the constraints of both language and
our bodies. The term Kabbalah comes from the Hebrew
"to receive." Through various doctrines and techniques,
many of which were secret, practitioners sought a higher
state of consciousness. The Old Testament book of Eze-
kial describes a celestial chariot swooping down from the
heavens. Only the initiated and schooled were allowed to
seek such transcendence since, without proper training

and preparation, its exercise could be physically dangerous (madness, death, apostasy).

Abraham ben Samuel Abulafia (1240-1292) was of the mystical tradition, and armed with the fearlessness of faith, publicly declared that he was on his way to Rome to convert Pope Nicholas III to Judaism. The pope was not amused, condemned Abulafia to death, and prepared a stake at which he was to be burned. But the pope died in the night, suggesting to some that Abulafia had a direct pipeline to the forces of the universe.

Many of the Kabbalah texts are unapologetically erotic, as the sexual union between husband and wife can be highly spiritual. (In twentieth-century literature Hemingway writes about sex causing the earth to move, and some commentators interpret his short story "Cross-Country Snow" as a sexual allegory). The tradition of the Kabbalah recognizes, as do all who try with words to describe the transcendent, that the task is impossible. That is why rituals and procedures obtain. One of those is strengthening the body as a necessity for strengthening the soul. Health is not just the absence of disease, but an overall state of well-being enhanced by a communion with nature.

Nineteenth-century Rabbi Nachman of Bratslav is quoted as saying that everything man is afraid of is within himself just as everything he craves is there, too. The Hebrew word for this is devekuth—an inner peace so ecstatic and detached as to erase earthly cares. Such a journey has no road map, no clear destination and no native guides. It is what psychologist Abraham Maslow in the twentieth-century described as a "peak experience."

Kabbalah has endured the split personality of reverence for tradition on the one hand and a kind of mystical/ spiritual anarchy on the other. Said the sixteenth-century mystic Isaac Luria (known as the Lion): "How shall I express what my soul has received?" The answer is that there isn't an answer.

A twentieth-century interpreter of Kabbalah was Martin Buber, who started out as a mystic, evolved into an existentialist, and concluded as a relationalist. His 1923 book I and Thou distinguishes between the I-It relationship that treats the other as a thing, and the I-Thou relationship, where there is a total giving of one's being to the other. The I-Thou relationship is reminiscent of Aristotle's virtuous friendship of two who are both enlightened and have discovered moderation in all things. Buber's I-Thou can exist not just between people but also with art, nature, and all that is. Critical to Buber's theology (and to the mysticism of skiing, I would add) is being open and receptive to the experiences of the universe. Our relationship with nature, he says, clings beneath the threshold of speech. We can feel the breath of the eternal thou in a context that contains neither time nor space.

The Land of Beyond

ROBERT SERVICE (1874-1958)

Have you ever heard of the Land of Beyond,
That dreams at the gates of the day?
Alluring it lies at the skirts of the skies,
And ever so far away;
Alluring it calls: O ye the yoke galls,
And ye of the trail overfond,
With saddle and pack, by paddle and track,
Let's go to the Land of Beyond!
Have ever you stood where the silences brood,
And vast the horizons begin,
At the dawn of the day to behold far away
The goal you would strive for and win?
Yet ah! In the night when you gain to the height,
With the vast pool of heaven star-spawned,
Afar and agleam, like a valley of dream,
Still mocks you a Land of Beyond.
Thank God! There is always a Land of Beyond
For us who are true to the trail;
A vision to seek, a beckoning peak,
A farness that never will fail;
A pride in our soul that mocks at a goal,
A manhood that irks at a bond,
And try how we will, unattainable still,
Behold it, our Land of Beyond!

CHAPTER 16

Old Soles

I won't be old 'til my feet hurt, and my feet
only hurt when I don't let 'em dance enough,
so I'll keep on dancing.

—BILL "BOJANGLES" ROBINSON

I was sitting at the bar of the Peacock at 8:30 on a Sunday morning (and yes, it is a notorious Corvallis dive; and no, I wasn't drinking alcohol). The Willamette river was too high for us to row, and I didn't want to endure the torture, boredom, self-loathing, and general depression resulting from an hour and a half of erging. The ergometer (Concept II rowing machine) is a torture device, and don't let anyone tell you otherwise. Pancakes seemed like a better way to go.* There are no strangers sitting at the bar on Sunday morning. Turns out one guy on my right was from Klamath Falls, where I once found a paring knife on the football field as I got up out of the mud, and the other guy, big hat and all, was a trail rider who appreciated horses more than humans and was annoyed that riders of another outfit were not keeping up the trails and campgrounds.

I thought, "What the hell," and asked Big Hat what was the strangest thing that had happened to him in the wilderness. He puzzled, stroked his chin in cowboy fashion, and told me that they were compass riding and looking for skulls for his collection at Fort Rock. Fort Rock is a huge crescent-shaped geological phenomenon southeast of Bend, Oregon, formed—some speculate—in as little as a month, by swirling, blowing volcanic dust and debris. It has been inhabited for millennia by hunters and wanderers, and an exquisite pair of woven sandals dating back 9,500 years was found there and is now at the Museum of Natural and Cultural History at the University of Oregon.

Skulls were in short supply that day, but he came upon a large white saucer-like thing that caused him to dismount and investigate. Turns out it was a mushroom that had been nibbled by mice and other rodents and maybe deer; and when he pulled it out, the stem was "six inches long." The pre-nibbling cap must have been "as big as a dinner plate, and out there where this is, there is no water. Amazing." My pancakes arrived.

As I chewed, I pondered what the soul has to do with this whole question of our wonder and appreciation of nature and its metaphysical embrace. Which of course led me to remember Jim Harrang, who possesses the best name for a lawyer of anyone I have ever known. Jim fought with the Tenth Mountain Division in World War II and was as resistant to changing his style as anyone, so in the early 1970s you could spot him on the slopes because he was the only one still skiing the reverse shoulder method. He got down the mountain just fine, and when he stopped, you could check out his leather boots when everyone else had switched to plastic.

Jim and his law partner, Art Johnson, also an excellent skier, were in Sun Valley, and Jim had to get his bindings checked. The way they did it then was that one guy would stand on the back of your skis, and you would dive over this leather-covered sawhorse, and presumably your bindings would release. So Jim took a dive or two and nothing happened, and the technician told him to dive—which he did, ripping the leather soles off both of his boots. On that day he became the not-so-proud owner of a new pair of plastic boots.

Another instance of the sole being good for the soul was my daily trek down to get the morning paper. We lived on a mountainside outside Bozeman up a steep quarter-mile of road with three switchbacks. I loved the winter there—couldn't get enough of it. The snow would swirl off the roof of the house during a storm, and Vladimir, our lovely big, white Samoyed, would trudge along behind me as I ran the snowblower to clear our driveway. Vladimir, and his sidekick Doctor Jerry, also a Samoyed, would choose to lie in the snow even if there were a clear patch on the deck. The third of the canine crew was Isabel, a black standard poodle who fancied that she was in charge.

Once the driveway was cleared, out came the plastic sled, the goggles and overpants. I already had on my Sorels, with the aforementioned soles. I would sit on the sled, feet spread forward, and launch off down the road, all three dogs barking along and trying to bite me as we flew. I could steer, sort of, with the soles of my boots, although more than once I went shooting off into the ditch. It was a rollicking good way to start the day as was the run back up the hill with the paper in hand. What's not to love about winter?

*The Peacock was famous for its 2,2,and 2 breakfast—2 eggs, 2 carbs (toast, pancakes or hash browns), and 2 meat (bacon strips, sausage, or ham). When I took my rowing partner Jack Elder there after a practice one morning, I ordered eggs, pancakes and bacon but he didn't want meat so told the waitress to leave it off. When the checks came, mine was the advertised $1.99 and Jack's was $4.00. "What's this," he exclaimed. "You pay extra for the substitution," she said in a tone that invited no rejoinder.

CHAPTER 17

Jay Bowerman

Nothing great was ever done without
much enduring.

—SAINT CATHERINE OF SIENA

A uthor's note: Jay Bowerman was an Olympic biathlete
and, for twenty-six years, the naturalist, Nature Center
honcho, and environmental conscience of Sunriver, the
celebrated, nature-friendly resort in Central Oregon. He
has written over twenty scientific papers on amphibians,
specifically the spotted frog, and picks a pretty mean banjo.
I asked Jay and Jonathan Chaffee (Chapter 27), both elite
athletes who have spent a lifetime on skis, to reflect on the
inward journey—the moments of euphoria and despair
and the self-knowledge their interactions with nature have
brought.

Here is Jay's response:

First off, it's worth mentioning that when you're talking about what a cross-country skier experiences during a
race, the experience is generally different if you're talking
with an elite skier versus the "less-than-elite" skier. A study
published a number of years ago, which I believe came out

of Ken Cooper's aerobics lab [the Cooper Aerobics Center], looked at some of the psychological elements of distance runners. They studied a lot of runners of all levels up to and including the likes of Kenny Moore, Frank Shorter and Steve Prefontaine.

The nonelite runners frequently spoke of having a song or some kind of "distraction" that they focused on during a 10k race that took their mind off their fatigue or "pain" level. Not so for the elite runners, who actually reported focusing sharply on everything they were feeling. This difference may be one of the factors that helps make elite athletes perform better. Whether or not pain was involved isn't the issue. Pain is part of the deal for everybody. Those who reach the elite level have to be acutely aware of everything their system is doing. Whether it is runners, skiers, cyclists, or violinists, there is a combination of detachment and awareness that allows them to shut out everything that doesn't matter.

Another train of thought that came up when I spoke with Jon Chaffee earlier tonight is that during a cross-country ski race, a variety physiological effects can impact what one is experiencing. Oxygen debt and lactic acid buildup begins to alter the blood chemistry in addition to affecting the sensation in the muscles. As the pH of the blood drops, this affects the brain, although I can't tell you in what way.

The second effect comes from the release of endogenous hormones called endorphins, that, in the extreme, can produce a sensation of euphoria (think "runner's high") but more often just results in a feeling of calm and well-being following a sustained aerobic workout. Third, there is the issue of blood sugar which, in a sustained effort, can ultimately drop precipitously to the point that the athlete cannot push hard enough to be breathing hard because the muscles just refuse to respond. In the world of aerobic competition, this is referred to as "bonking," and Jon was sort of legendary for his ability to push into that zone.

Finally, there is simple "oxygen debt" in which the exertion leads to forcing muscles to begin functioning anaerobically because the effort level is burning calories faster than the delivery of oxygen to the muscles can sustain the conversion of glycogen to glucose. All of the factors mentioned above probably come into play in affecting the mental state of the athlete, and experiencing these is often different in training than in racing.

Having said all of that, however, let's consider some of the ideas you threw out. Do we experience "out-of-body" sensations? Indeed, and in various ways. Pure fatigue, lactate buildup, may be sufficient to explain a sensation of "tunnel vision" that many of us have experienced late in a long race or workout. It is an odd sensation in which the mind stays focused on a fairly small circle that seems to be illuminated straight ahead with nearly everything more than a few degrees "off-center" becoming fuzzy and indistinct, and it applies not only to what one sees but also what we hear. The world just gets narrower.

There is also a strange sensation that one experiences on those rare occasions when everything comes together to produce an exceptional performance, and "out-of-body experience" is not a bad description. I can't speak for others, but it didn't happen often for me. One of the most vivid, however, was one that also involved Jon Chaffee. I was staying at Jon's parents' house while training and racing in New England prior to the "Hanover Relays" at Dartmouth

College. The snow conditions all week were exceptional, and I had several days of good training prior to the race weekend. It would be the biggest domestic race I was ever in.

The day before the actual competition, I went out for a final easy workout, and started just cruising comfortably around the 10-kilometer course to be completely familiar with it. The snow was so good and my wax was working perfectly so that I found myself powering up the uphills almost effortlessly and gliding fast on the downhills. The sensation was overwhelming, and I settled into a rhythm that had me flying around the course. Although I was acutely aware of each turn, each uphill and downhill, I lost complete track of time and distance, came flying through at the end of 10 kilometers feeling so good that without thinking headed right back out on the course. The next thing I realized was that I was completing 20 kilometers and thought to myself "that wasn't exactly a smart thing to do the day before a race." But I was definitely feeling the "runner's high" and went back to the Chaffee house to a warm supper and slept well.

I was to ski with three other members of the US team, a first for me, with Jon to ski the opening leg which involves a "mass start" with more than 50 teams sprinting across a flat meadow before the tracks narrowed to two groomed tracks wide. I was scheduled to ski the third leg by which time our team should be in the lead and I could have an easy time of it before tagging the US's top cross-country racer. However, while we were warming up and testing waxes, about 10 minutes before race time, Jon came up and said he wasn't feeling all that hot and would I be willing to ski the first leg. I was a "freshman" on the team and had never been in a sprint start like that, but not knowing any better, I said, "Why not?"

There was a frantic flash of skis at the start, but as we approached the narrow tracks at the first long uphill, I found myself with only three or four skiers in front of me, and at every stride I was running up onto the tails of the skier ahead of me. Within 100 yards I was in the lead and just as the day before, my skis were perfect, the snow was perfect, and every part of the course was exactly as I'd seen it the day before and skiing felt effortless. I flew through the 10-kilometer with no sensation of time, pain, or fatigue—only pure focus on the track, squeezing everything out of each stride, turn, uphill, downhill. I never looked back to see who was behind me—just had a sensation of feeling like my skis, poles, arms, and legs were willing to do whatever I asked. I reached the end of the loop, tagged our next skier, and had nearly 2½ minutes of recovery before the next skier came through. I've never asked Jon whether he was really feeling uncertain that day or if maybe he and John Caldwell had put me in first out of some sense that this was a good time to "baptize" me.

I had a similar sensation again one day when I was doing summer foot training on McKenzie View Drive near home [Springfield, Oregon]. I had planned on running a six-mile time trial on the road. Training had been going well. There were mile-markers along the road, which I used to check my pace. I had planned on hitting a particular pace that would be close to a personal best for me over a six-mile distance. There was a headwind on the three miles "going out" on the road, but then I would have a tailwind after making the turn at the end of the road and heading back.

I found myself comfortably hitting my times over the first three miles so was confident I would finish the time trial at or below my personal best. I was running completely alone on a beautiful, mostly level country road under large maple trees. I made the turn at three miles ten-seconds-under-pace, and now with the wind at my back fairly flew back the final three miles. Again, I had no sensation of the passage of time despite the fact that I was tracking my one-mile split times the entire way. Consciously, I knew exactly how much time had gone by, but at the subconscious level, it was more like when we dream and don't actually feel the passage of time. I think I took another thirty seconds off my expected time over the second three miles; and although I was running hard, in a way it felt effortless.

There are also the opposite sensations. I've been in races and workouts where things just plain don't work, where one has to will each and every stride. And again sometimes one has the feeling that you're outside, watching yourself. I think those events likely contribute to a recurring nightmare that I (and I suspect others) have of dreaming I'm in a race and have to keep willing my legs to move and they barely do. Teresa tells me later when I have this dream, although it isn't as obvious to her as when I kicked hard at a German shepherd in a dream the other night and nearly knocked her out of bed. I've heard other people talk about dreaming they're being chased and their legs won't move, but for me, it is always a ski race or footrace.

CHAPTER 18

Klutzi Kid

Anything you are good at contributes to happiness.
—BERTRAND RUSSELL, philosopher

Todd Tokes has the voice you always wish you had—that mellifluous, articulate, trustworthy narrator of life as it should be. He is the voice-over of commercials, documentaries, and testimonials—the Walter Cronkite of trust and community. "I was always the last kid chosen for any sport when I was in school," he told me. "I was the Charlie Brown of the comics—except it was my life, and my self-confidence was constantly challenged."

Now he is an ambassador at the Mt. Bachelor resort, which means he is around—at the top of the lift, on the mountain, in the lodge-- helping skiers who are not familiar with the mountain, providing information, spreading good cheer. "There is peace and solace on the mountain that you cannot find anywhere else," he says. "You can find your own level of expertise in skiing and challenge yourself. I wasn't sought-after for any sport in school. Maybe I am still catching up, but I can go out by myself and challenge myself and conquer new slopes and have real success at this stage in my life and spread the joy of that accomplishment to others. As a former klutz you finally find your way, and there is a tremendous renewal in that. There is the solitude and peace of the mountain and hope for all the kids who were never any good in sports."

Mark Hamby has skied every year at Mt. Bachelor since 1958—the year it opened. He didn't weigh enough at age seven to ride the Poma lift, so the rope tow had to do. He has taught skiing since 1974 and says that for the last seven years that he taught middle school, he came home every day with a headache, but that never happens after a day teaching skiing.

"There is something called the golden hour from about three to four o'clock on a stormy day when the clouds on the horizon part and the sun rakes the slopes and the wind stops," he says. "The mountain becomes a great cathedral. I love the last hour." It does seem to be the way of the mountain. The day is a stormy, windy whiteout until that last hour, and then the sun appears and taunts you just as the lifts are closing. Perhaps this is the mountain's invitation to come back again tomorrow.

> *The sun reserves*
> *the prize of the horizon for the few*
> *who know it can never be won.*
>
> —SAMUEL HAZO,
> "Listening to What Was Here"

Mark likes teaching kids the most. They are the easiest, the fastest learners, and for the most part, the ones who complain the least. One time, though, he was riding the lift with a kid who said he was not feeling so good—a little queasy. Mark zips up the boy's jacket, puts his arm around him, and—blech—the kid throws up into his parka. They get off at the top of the lift, unzip the jacket, and out falls the steaming yucky mess onto the boy's boots.

Barfs notwithstanding, Mark says: "I wouldn't mind if it were winter year-round."

Same with Ty Wolfe and Mason Tour, a couple of boarders who are out there shredding almost every day. They say they have the reverse of Seasonal Affective Disorder (SAD). During the summer, they would like to go into some restaurant's cooler and watch ski videos all day. Standing inside the ski shop at Mt. Bachelor, Ty says, "I will make a big sweeping turn and look back at the track on the slope and say to myself, 'This is why I was put on this earth.'"

The young woman listening behind the repair counter remarks, "Your eyes are glowing right now, Ty." Ty and Mason are getting into the spirit of the spirit now and they recite, almost like a church litany, "you can't explain it or anticipate it—that spiritual thing just hits you sometimes. You're not ready for it, don't expect it, but it is real." And then there's heli-skiing. Every run is really good, untracked, and unknown. You say to yourself, "Is that a cliff? Should I jump off it?" The answer usually is, "Yes." [I suspect if the answer were "no," we wouldn't be having this conversation].

But Mason says that he doesn't ride as aggressively as he used to when he would routinely scare himself. "Now I try to fine-tune it—do perfect turns and find the powder where the wind left it," he says, adding, "The wind makes it different even though we know everything that is on this mountain."

Loving the wind would not be the sentiment of most skiers.

CHAPTER 19

Prinoth Bison Groomer

Winter is not a season; it is an occupation.

—SINCLAIR LEWIS, writer

Over 100 inches of snow buried Mt. Bachelor in the last two weeks, and they are still trying to catch up with it, but who is to complain; snow is what this sport craves. And pushing it around, grooming it like a giant white lawn, and keeping the skiers happy (read, not leaving death cookies* on the runs) is what it is all about.

Let's start with the machine itself. It is a Prinoth Bison with sixty-six-inch steel tracks, a plow on the front that can be manipulated twelve different ways with wings on either side and a tiller on the back that, like the fingers on a hand, can groom multiple patterns. The driver sits on the starboard side of the cabin and moves a lever with the left hand that controls the tracks. It has brakes, but the revolution of the tracks is what really controls the machine's speed.

The driver's right hand is on a joy stick that has multiple buttons to control the front blade and the tiller. When the snow is wet (and it often is on Mt. Bachelor), the blade curls it up and over in front of the machine like a breaking ocean wave. When it is snowing hard, the yard-long windshield wipers do their best, but often the spotlight on the roof of the cab is needed to see where the hell you are going.

I rode along with Eric Gilliland, the supervisor of the midnight to eight o'clock crew of eight operators driving eight machines. They assemble before the shift and plan how to attack the three thousand acres of the hill. Eric says it is like a puzzle to get everything groomed so there aren't ridges, the roads connect, and the whole hill gets done (or at least as much as the conditions allow—sometimes it is deep enough that the machine won't go uphill with the tiller going).

Eric has been grooming for 15 years and has worked in the ski industry ever since college, starting out selling tickets, working in the parking lot, doing whatever needed to be done until he got a chance to drive a plow and then a groomer. He likes the solitude of being out on the mountain alone; and if he wants to ski, his work is done just in time for first tracks.

How do you learn to drive one of these beasts? He first drove one at Tamarack Resort near McCall, Idaho. The boss gave him some quick verbal instruction, hopped out, and said, "Let's go." Eric's machine slipped off a track and headed down the hill at thirty miles per hour toward the trees. He finally got the blade around and stopped. "I didn't enjoy that," he said to himself; but as he became more confident and more proficient, he came to think those slides were kind of fun.

What isn't fun is not being able to see ten feet in front of the machine in a whiteout. It is easy to get disoriented, to not be able to find landmarks, no matter how well one knows the mountain, and to slip off the roads, which he did once way around the mountain about as far as one can get from the lodge. He couldn't go down because there were too many trees, so he worked his way up only to slip off the road again, and this time he was against trees and had to call for help.

Another time, grooming at Mt. Hood Meadows near the Express Chair that parallels the Blue Chair, the visibility was zero and he was next to a big drop-off. He had his face up against the windshield terrified that he was going too fast and would sail off into oblivion. He put his blade down to slow his speed, started to put the tracks in reverse, and realized that he had been stopped the whole time. He didn't know for how long.

What is the strangest thing you have seen on the mountain? "This was at Meadows, and there is some difference of opinion about what we saw," Eric says. "It was night, and there were seven or eight machines grooming together in a line as we climbed up the mountain. It, whatever it was, came straight at us.

"It was the biggest, brightest flaming object I have ever seen, and it disappeared and crashed behind the mountain. Everyone was on the radio saying what was that, what did you see, and after a while we all began to doubt what our eyes and our brains had told us."

How about animals? "There are pine martens—you see their tracks under the chairs, looking to scarf up any snacks that have been dropped. There are foxes whose coats are black or grey-black, and they have been around for years, so they apparently can make a living on the high mountain.

JOHN FROHNMAYER

Then there are crows that hang out around the lodge and an occasional great horned owl. That's pretty much it."

During my ride-along, Eric got a call from the driver of a wheeled forklift who needed some help delivering his load to the deck of the Sunrise Lodge. Eric plowed up a roadway through the snow but worried that it was pretty soft because of the moisture level. The forklift, on four big tires, got up without difficulty, deposited its load and backed down smartly until its down-slope rear tire sank, and the whole machine began to sway and yaw. The driver skillfully managed to right the ship, design a new angle, and get down to the parking lot. All in a night's work.

At the end of the shift, Eric got a call from the ski patrol supervisor checking in on the status of the grooming and wanting to know if they could begin putting up their signs to designate trails and warn skiers of obstacles. Eric advised him of half a dozen places where a hole, a rock or a stump needed marking with a pole to warn skiers away. And with that, another night's work was done.

* A sign of good grooming is the absence of death cookies—those big chunks of ice that can grab your ski tip and send you into an atomic face-plant. Eric was the Prince of the Prinoth. Not a death cookie in sight.

CHAPTER 20

Grace

> Our own body possesses a wisdom which
> we who inhabit the body lack. We give it orders
> which make no sense.
>
> —HENRY MILLER, writer

E instein told us that past and future are illusions and only the present moment exists. So when you are standing on the cornice, and there is nowhere you would rather be and no direction to go but down, you are one with the universe—you are the universe. Time has vanished. Earthly cares and troubles are gone. There is nothing but air beneath you, and you take that leap of faith, both actual and virtual, and embrace the everlasting. Then you hit, and had better make the first turn to gain some actual control. A state of grace such as this may last but a moment, but the euphoria can energize you for a lifetime.

The beautiful moves in curves. It is true in art. It is true in religion. It is true in sport. Sure anybody can go straight down the mountain, and the shortest distance between two points is still a straight line, but what is beautiful is the lithe body, the smooth efficient movement, the quiet torso, the effortless compression, the flawless arc of the track. The term sprezzatura—effortless grace—is from the Italian poet and diplomat Baldassare Castiglione's 1528 Book of the Courtier. There is also a Greek word, kalokagathia, which means beauty and nobility of soul.

Grace is honoring others while at the same time honoring one's self. It is a reaffirmation of the me by making it secondary to the immediacy of others. "How are you?" can be a question rather than just a greeting. The effortless part is the key, both in sport and in personal relations. The harder you work at grace the worse you do. One has to abandon. Let go. The German poet Schiller said, "Grace is the beauty of form under the influence of freedom."

Grace eludes clear definition almost as much as the words mystical and transcendent. It can be sensual. It can be dynamic. It can be forceful or gentle—but generally it is loose, not tight; elastic, not rigid; light, not ponderous; terse, not wordy. The great legal lecturer Irving Younger identified the difference between grace and mere ability by describing Willie Mays as running in on a fly ball, then back, and making a spectacular over the shoulder basket catch, whereas Joe DiMaggio always seemed to be where the ball was going to come down, tapping his glove once, and making the catch. Slugger and rival Ted Williams said DiMaggio even looked good striking out. He didn't run—he seemed to glide hardly touching the grass.

Arthur Mitchell, founder of the Dance Theatre of Harlem, created some incredibly beautiful pieces, and even his company's curtain calls were full of grace. At the end of one piece, to the insistent infusion of African drums, the lead dancer would turn to the line on the right, to the line on the left, tap his staff twice and come forward with a move I can't even begin to describe. Those bows alone were worth the price of admission. Years later when Arthur was on the National Council on the Arts, I recalled that Portland performance, and he repeated the move in suit and street shoes. Sprezzatura.

> *What a piece of work is a man, …*
> *in form and moving how express and admirable.*
> —SHAKESPEARE, "Hamlet," act 2, scene 2

Not always. Dr. William B. Long III, an emergency physician at Legacy Emanuel Medical Center in Portland, and his father—also a physician—were attending a medical convention and, during a break on the street outside the lecture hall, playing "spot the lesion" in which they would try to diagnose a malady by looking at how a person walked. They saw one man walking particularly awkwardly and made their diagnoses only to find the same man sitting near them at lunch. So they gave their opinions, and the man, also a physician, said: "Well, all three of us were wrong. I thought it was a fart."

Poet, singer, and philosopher Leonard Cohen, thought to be the preeminent Canadian poet of his generation, and not incidentally, the composer of Suzanne and Hallelujah, two of the very best songs of the twentieth century, described his life's path as "wide and without direction." Asked what he meant, he said when he wakes up each morning, he asks himself whether he is in a state of grace— whether he has the balance to ride out the chaos around him. It isn't a question of trying to change the world; that would be "arrogant and warlike." It is a feeling of being smooth, like a ski going over a hill.

There is a piece of reverence in grace. Reverence and humility. These are conditions necessary for receiving the mystical because they acknowledge that most of what is given us is not of our own making. It is a condition of thankfulness, empathy, compassion and awe. It is the music of the soul.

For what is life but reaching for an answer?
And what is death but a refusal to grow?

—MARY OLIVER, "Magellan"

The question arises: If we are thankful, must it be to a god? What if there is no one on the other end of the line? My response is, it doesn't matter. We can be grateful just to be alive. We can be grateful for nature and to be a part of nature. That's enough.

CHAPTER 21

Darrell at 93

How old would you be if you didn't know
how old you were?

—SATCHEL PAIGE, baseball great

A rtificial barriers don't exist on the mountain. Your wealth, education, social station, or religion are irrelevant to the snow, the trees, and the gravity. Ability does matter. Age, not so much, at least not in Darrell Price's case. He is 93 and on holiday from time.

Darrell is one of a group of scoundrels who gather to tell lies to one another in the Sunrise Lodge at Mt. Bachelor before the lifts open. They get their boots on; go to the john; don gloves, helmets, and parkas; and go out to ski. Fast. Thing about Darrell is that he doesn't see or hear too well, so you want him in front of you so he doesn't ski up and clean you out as he did to one of the stalwarts last season.

Darrell has some property in Northern California. Several summers ago, one of his houses needed a roof, so he put it on. By himself. "Did you carry those seventy-pound bundles up the ladder yourself?" He nods. We shake our heads. He drives his truck up to the mountain each morning and sometimes will take a little nap in the cab if he is early. The patch on his parka says, "90+ Club." Membership defines the word exclusive.

He says, "Just go down; anything you do is good for a 93-year-old." But he can ski. We went off the Summit Chair last season and out into the west bowl, and he was cutting turns in the powder nonstop. He skis kind of bow-legged; but hey, he stays up, usually. The other day he was skiing with the scoundrels, and he knew a jump was coming up— "But I never knew I was going to jump it until I was in the air," he says. "I landed on my face. When I stopped, I put my hand to my cheek and said to myself, 'What happened?' I decided I was alright, and the fellows brought me my skis and poles." He went into the lodge to inventory his body parts and was back on the hill the next day.

There is a run the guys call "Darrell's Dinger" because there is a prominent rock that Darrell hit twice the same day. Some years ago he was skiing the high traverse toward the west bowl off of the summit just below one of the big rock faces. He tried to do a jump turn, came out of both bindings and slid headfirst down "about a football field and a half." No damage.

I asked Darrell if he did any more roofing last summer. He allowed as how he did, but he cut the bundles in half so he was only carrying thirty-five pounds up the ladder. One must make some concessions to age.

Fifteen years younger than Darrell, I learned to ski my last year in high school. Learned is not entirely accurate. My friends took me to the top of the lift and said that if I got going too fast I should just fall down. We rented our skis in those days from Art Ekerson's Rogue Ski Shop in Medford, and they were long—210 cm—wooden jobbers with metal edges. We started, of course, with two, but routinely would bring back three and sometimes four pieces. Bindings were cables that went around a groove in the back of our leather boots. There was a swivel piece on the toe that released sometimes.

Lesson-free learning was a bad way to begin skiing. For years, and even sometimes today, those bad habits of stiff knees, turning back into the mountain, arms flying up in the air, and sitting back still return, always at the most critical times. Take lessons to learn; that is my advice. Friends are for drinks after the skiing is done.

Trips down the mountain in the "blood wagon" were common in those days when I was learning (not me, thankfully). Two or three times a day we would see the patrollers, one ahead and one behind the sled snowplowing down the mountain on their way to the first aid station. It was worth watching to see if the injured skier, whose face was covered with a tarp, was about to experience a second bone-insulting event.

Terry Telford, one of the scoundrels and a Vietnam War helicopter pilot who survived six shoot-downs and is of acerbic good humor, tells of the safety bindings they used when he first started racing in high school. They had bear-trap side bindings with a French wrap—a long leather thong that went around and around the boot. Skis were wood, and the safety feature was short screws. If the screws ripped out on a particularly aerobic fall, they each had a pocket full of longer screws and a file to take off the tips if they went through the base of the ski.

My first pair of metal skis were Head Standards that I got for Christmas in 1961. They were black just like dial phones used to be, 210 cm long with my name engraved in white just in front of the cable bindings. I put on my ski boots, locked into the bindings, and tried to do a kick turn in the living room, falling backwards, sweeping a lamp off the table on my way to flattening the Christmas tree.

Pat, whom I met in the Sunrise Lodge, said his eight-year-old granddaughter told him she wanted to learn to ski. He was sixty-three and recently retired, so he said that if she took lessons, he would, too. Now, five years later, they are both loving it. Age only matters if it matters.

A metaphor that is meaningful to me is that while the sides and the bottom of a clay pot are tactile and visible, it is the space inside that contains the treasure. Such is the nature of community. It is often circumscribed by boundaries—physical, relational, ethnic, geographic—but what holds it together is common experience, kinship, or a sense of shared history. So while the people who ski are as different as the people who walk down the street (even more different because some who ski can't walk) what makes them—us—a community is the shared experience of sliding on snow, letting gravity do its thing, and reveling in the speed and the quiet and the majesty of the mountain.

You Are Old, Father William

FROM ALICE'S ADVENTURES IN WONDERLAND
LEWIS CARROLL (1832-1898)

"You are old, Father William," the young man said,
"And your hair has become very white;
And yet you incessantly stand on your head—
Do you think, at your age, it is right?"
"In my youth," Father William replied to his son,
"I feared it might injure my brain;
But now that I'm perfectly sure I have none,
Why, I do it again and again."

"You are old," said the youth, "as I mentioned before,
And have grown most uncommonly fat;
Yet you turned a back-somersault in at the door—
Pray, what is the reason of that?"
"In my youth," said the sage, as he shook his grey locks,
"I kept all my limbs very supple
By the use of this ointment—one shilling per box—
Allow me to sell you a couple."

"You are old," said the youth, "and your jaws are too
weak
For anything tougher than suet;
Yet you finished the goose, with the bones and the
beak—
Pray, how did you manage to do it?"

JOHN FROHNMAYER

"In my youth," said his father, "I took to the law,
And argued each case with my wife;
And the muscular strength, which it gave to my jaw,
Has lasted the rest of my life."

"You are old," said the youth, "one would hardly
suppose
That your eye was as steady as ever;
Yet you balanced an eel on the end of your nose—
What made you so awfully clever?"
"I have answered three questions and that is enough,"
Said his father; "don't give yourself airs!
Do you think I can listen all day to such stuff?
Be off, or I'll kick you downstairs!"

CHAPTER 22

Because You Can

Life ain't no dress rehearsal.

—TALLULAH BANKHEAD, actress

Mysticism converges with skiing because both require mind over matter. Henry Ford said that those who think they can and those that think they can't are both right. Skiing requires that you conquer the obstacles: the pitch, the bumps, the trees (you are supposed to miss them), the weather, the light. The mountain will cut you no slack; it might even kill you. Should you be afraid? Probably. Will you conquer your fear? Absolutely. That is the transformative moment—when you decide, "I can do this"—and 100 percent of the people on the mountain have done that. "It is about overcoming fear," a guy on the chair told me, "and there is always a new challenge, a new scary pitch, or a course through the trees to keep the edge of my fear alive. I love that."

> *He is no fugitive—escaped, escaping.*
> *No one has seen him stumble looking back.*
> *His fear is not behind him but beside him*

On either hand to make his course perhaps
A crooked straightness yet no less a straightness.
He runs face forward. He is a pursuer.
He seeks a seeker who in his turn seeks
Another still, lost far into the distance.
Any who seek him seek in him the seeker.
His life is a pursuit of a pursuit forever.
It is the future that creates his present.
All is an interminable chain of longing.

—ROBERT FROST,

"Escapist–Never"

Fellow scoundrel Chris Hieatt taught math in the Los Angeles area for a career and coached track and field after school. He is a fine athlete and tells of a kid who had a severe stuttering problem. Chris would stretch with him, and then start jogging. After a while Chris would toss out easy questions that just required a yes or no answer, and then they would run, and the more they ran, the better the young man's speech became until eventually he was conversing without difficulty. It wouldn't last forever, but it would propel him into regular speech for a while after the practice had ended. Life is about obstacles, but obstacles come in lots of different packages.

Oregon Adaptive Sports has a big presence on Mount Bachelor. You see volunteers and coaches, many wearing the distinctive orange vest, working with seated skiers, with low-vision skiers, with those who simply need a companion to ski safely. They serve people with cognitive, physical, and emotional deficits. Kadee Mardula is the on-mountain operations director. She has a master's degree in mechanical engineering and got into this field with the hope of designing and building prosthetics for athletes. She says risk is important for growth. An athlete herself, her work has helped her identify why she craves that extra thrill. Like so many others who work with people with disabilities, she is inspired by the determination and guts of these athletes.

"We treat each person as a person first," Kadee says. "Adaptive techniques are important, and our coaches and volunteers learn some of those, but most important is to see the real person, not just the disability." People learn differently, so the equipment and style of instruction have to fit. "We are dedicated to a fully inclusive community where our athletes can play and challenge themselves with all of the rest of us," she says. "Snow, water, and gravity are great equalizers, and our athletes are some of the most motivated people you will ever meet."

A high school OAS athlete just returned to the locker room. His companion says he is as solid as a rock on his skis. "I didn't do anything but chase him down the mountain." Another athlete who had just started boarding was progressing so quickly that he was already talking flips and jumps. Leah Perischilli is an OAS instructor with a background as a professional patroller and mom. She reads up on her student's experiences and abilities during the ride up to the mountain, and adapts the day's learning accordingly. She sees the growth and the joy of breaking boundaries and the personal empowerment the whole process brings. For some, just getting one's ski clothes on is a challenge; for others, their goal is total independence. "Our youngest is three and oldest, ninety-two," Leah says, "and for me, it is the universal love of watching their achievements. People with disabilities are often on the fringe. Their joy when they link their first turns is as great as if they had summited Everest."

The sit skiers usually start on a bi-ski. These units, which can cost around $5,000, have two skis for easier balance and outrigger ski poles. The athlete is tethered around the waist with leads held by a trailing skier on either side to prevent runaways. A third volunteer skis ahead to show the way. Change of direction is by shifting body weight, and as skiers get the hang of it, they can progress to a mono-ski. The poles have little skis on them for turning and stopping. To see a seated mono-skier carving down the mountain is a real thing of beauty.

Kadee says she is thrilled with the progress of one particular female athlete who now not only mono-skis, but in the off-season is rushing full speed at the out-of-doors on an adaptive mountain bike. One of Kadee's robotics professors at Oregon State University remembered her fondly: "You have to be motivated to motivate others," he said.

CHAPTER 23

Taoism

The further one goes, the less one knows.

—LAO-TZU

Taoism deals with essence—defined as the science of the mind—and with life—the science of the body. Taoists seek to enhance human existence, focusing on vitality, energy, and spirit. Each of these three centers of human existence has two parts: the abstract (the philosophical term is noumenon) and the temporal—that which we can see, move, and feel.

Vitality is associated with creativity and sexuality; energy with power and movement; and spirit with consciousness, thought, and reflection. The energy aspect of Taoism has led to exercise regimens, both ancient and modern, such as Tai Chi (absolute boxing), and healing arts such as massage and acupressure. Physical training strengthens both the body and the mind.

Taoism also has mental exercises designed to groom the mind, to empty it of extraneous thoughts, and to achieve a state of nothingness. The primary text, attributed to the founder Lao-tzu and probably compiled between 500 and

300 BCE, champions the union of vitality and conscious-ness with the strong and purified body leading to the agile and capable mind. When the spirit controls the body, the body obeys. When the body overrules the spirit, the spirit becomes exhausted.

Like many Western philosophies, Taoism identifies a "golden mean" that avoids excess, indulgence, and extravagance. The yin and yang balance each other as is visually portrayed by the divided circle with black and white shadings.

The concept of opposites interacting and dynamically balancing invites intuitive wisdom as a liberation from the rational world. Reason is fallible. Reason is limited. Reason will not make men wise. Indeed, when one sets out to accomplish something, one should start with the opposite: "Be bent and you will be straight."

Taoists concentrate on observation of nature to discern the characteristics of the Tao, and they urge a nimble, intui-tive spontaneity to react to nature's constant flux. The name for the Taoist temple means "to look."

Here are three excerpts from the Tao-te Ching of Lao-tzu:

Attain the climax of emptiness.

Returning to the root is called stillness:
Stillness is called return to life,
Return to life is called the constant;
Knowing the constant is called enlightenment.

When people are born they are supple,

and when they die they are stiff.
…Stiffness is thus a cohort of death,
flexibility is a cohort of life.

Similar to parables in the New Testament, the Tao is told in stories: a man's ax disappeared, and he observed that his neighbor's son was walking and acting like a thief. Then the man found his ax where he had mislaid it and noticed that the neighbor's son was no longer walking and acting like a thief.

The Tao is embraced by way of sincerity. It is fundamentally empty, yet it fills the universe. The body is the lotus root and the mind its bloom. Here is a portion of Ancestor Lu's "Hundred Character Tablet":

Yin and yang arise, alternating over and over again,
Everywhere producing the sound of thunder.
White clouds assemble on the summit,
Sweet dew bathes the polar mountain.
Having drunk the wine of longevity,
You wander free; who can know you?
You sit and listen to the stringless tune,
You clearly understand the mechanism of creation.
The whole of these twenty verses
Is a ladder straight to heaven.

Liu I-ming, a Taoist of the Ch'ing Dynasty probably born around 1737 CE, was a thought leader on both the ancient documents and those he created. The wisdom is clear but attribution is sometimes cloudy, so concentrate on the thought and not its author.

The natural Tao is calm, so heaven, earth, and myriad
beings
are born. The Tao of heaven and earth is penetrating
so yin
and yang prevail. Yin and yang push each other
onward,
and myriad changes go along.
Sages know the natural Tao cannot be violated.

Knowing others is intelligence,
Knowing yourself is true wisdom.
Mastering others is strength,
Mastering yourself is true power.

Those who know do not speak.
Those who speak do not know.

A man with outward courage dares to die;
A man with inward courage dares to live.

The Tao that can be told
is not the eternal Tao.
The name that can be named
is not the eternal name.

CHAPTER 24

That Indescribable Feeling

Great things are done when men and
mountains meet.

—WILLIAM BLAKE, poet

Or, if you would rather:

You will find no responsible man on top
of big mountains.

—DAVID LEE ROTH, singer

Maybe it is skiing Avalanche Bowl at Mount Bailey when the powder snow fluffs up over your head and you feel like you need a snorkel, or maybe it is the fifth hour of a cross-country endurance race when your mind goes on autopilot and your body is weightless, or maybe it is just the opposite—when your body and mind are in a shouting match: one screaming, "Enough!"; the other, "Not yet!"

Let's collect the descriptors: self-realization, fear, inner peace, awe, spiritual wonder, floating, gratefulness, pain, happiness, mindfulness, exhilaration, exhaustion, freedom, out of body, mystical, clarity, fun, and the list goes on because the feelings are individual and situational. Different individuals bring different experiences and expectations to the activity, and in the end, what I am talking about is not really describable in words anyway.

So why are you writing this, numbskull?

Let me transpose to a different key and try again. Jerry Magaro, yet another of the scoundrels and a clinical psychologist, skier, and dancer, says we can recognize things that are beyond our own reality and can benefit from them, acknowledge them, and practice them without being able to describe them. The lack of description doesn't make them any less real or any less valuable. Take meditation for example. With practice, there can be minutes and minutes of nothingness. There can be a sense of wonder like a child. There can be peace and serenity and lowered blood pressure.

According to writer Ursula Le Guin, "One of the functions of art is to give people the words to know their own experience. There are always areas of vast silence in any culture, and part of the artist's job is to go into those areas and come back from the silence with something to say."

Then there is the sense of being right with the place we are in—not disturbing nature, not crashing in with noise and bustle, but listening quietly, reverently, modestly. If we let nature speak to us, she will do so as family. We can be one with nature, but only on nature's terms, not our own. On a soulless seven-story cruise ship with casinos and dance bands, we have about as much chance of finding nature as on the equally soulless Las Vegas strip.

James Hillman, a poet and naturalist lovingly described as a "disruptive thinker," says that when tribal people set out to do something, they spend about 30 percent of their time getting things together and the rest in preparing and performing rituals, dances, prayers, and ceremonies. They do so to get into the right relationship with the natural world. They seek to walk in balance with the earth. It is a concept with which the modern "civilized" world is entirely unfamiliar. Our loss.

With skiing, particularly in the powder, a kind of weightlessness gives a sense of being outside of our bodies. We float, and we give off spontaneous whoops and shouts from the pure joy of it. These are wordless declarations of the freedom of our souls. We are in the moment; not thinking about doing the laundry, the sorrows of loss, or what's for dinner.

Vertigo is another kind of out-of-body experience. You are standing there in a whiteout and just fall over because you don't know which way is up—a total disorientation. It is a reduction rather than an enhancement of the senses. So part of what I am talking about is an ethereal space that is dynamic and ambiguous and perceived only obliquely. It could be either an expanded consciousness or a contracted one. It could be profound or pedestrian. It could touch our soul. It could produce physical emotion.

There is a condition at Mammoth Mountain in California called the windbuff. The wind swirls, and the snow flies around, and it is like skiing on air. With the snow filling your tracks and surrounding your waist so you can't see your skis, you are floating among the glimmering crystals that sparkle and fill your heart with gladness.

For others, the trees are the inspiration. One lady told me that she and her friends love to ski through the trees, the closer together the better. It makes her feel as if she were ten years old again. A boarder said the trees are speaking to him: "Riding through the trees is like being with my friends." The trees he is communing with are western hemlock, with a smattering of lodgepole and whitebark pine. All are very hard and unforgiving if you hit them. Friends act that way sometimes, too.

The mountain is a different world. A patroller responded to the question about a mystical experience by saying: "Yeah, I have one every morning when I get up here and watch the mountain turn pink and purple."

One Christmas morning in Bozeman we were sitting around opening presents when it had snowed twenty-three inches the night before, and we exclaimed in unison: "What are we doing here?" When we returned from one of the most exhilarating days ever, the neighbor had plowed our driveway.

The Snow Man

WALLACE STEVENS (1879-1955)

One must have a mind of winter
To regard the frost and the boughs
Of the pine-trees crusted with snow;

And have been cold a long time
To behold the junipers shagged with ice,
The spruces rough in the distant glitter

Of the January sun; and not to think
Of any misery in the sound of the wind,
In the sound of a few leaves,

Which is the sound of the land
Full of the same wind
That is blowing in the same bare place

For the listener, who listens in the snow,
And, nothing himself, beholds
Nothing that is not there and the nothing that
    is.

CHAPTER 25

Clearing the Mind

We can be absolutely certain only about things
we do not understand.

—ERIC HOFFER, philosopher

Just because we can't put it into words doesn't mean it isn't real. It is a primary lesson worth repeating. That we can't invent words to clothe it makes it more real, more compelling. Words do give humans power, no question about that. Genesis 2:20 describes how "Adam gave names to all cattle, and to the fowl of the air, and to every beast of the field." The sense of this allegory is power. The power to name is the power to control—the power of dominion over that which we can touch, feel, and see.

The sublime, the spiritual, and the ephemeral, on the other hand, don't have words and aren't subject to human dominion. But they are real, if we can create the space for them to enter at their own will and on their own terms into our lives. In his experience on Walden Pond, Henry David Thoreau was trying to create a space in his life for such spirituality by jettisoning most of what "civilized society" requires. "To affect the quality of the day, that is the highest of arts....Our life is frittered away by detail." Or, as put more bluntly by contemporary Toltec thinker Miguel Ruiz: "You eat their emotional garbage, and now it becomes your garbage."

So now I am going to propose some rules for aerobic meditation, to coin an oxymoron. Think of skiing as meditation where there is nothing but you and the mountain and the movement; nothing in the world. The energy is there—you just have to prepare yourself and your body to embrace it. This is a matter of witnessing on the one hand—being hyperalert—while, on the other hand, relaxing into a heightened state of awareness by looking inward. And you must believe in yourself.

Rule 1: Don't expend energy on things that do not matter. Right now the only thing that matters is a quiet mind. Put the rest of your life on a stage and close the curtain.

Rule 2: Concentrate on the process, not the outcome. This shouldn't be hard because you don't know what the outcome will be.

Rule 3: Eliminate distractions. One of the great lost opportunities for skiers is to plug in the headphones and absolutely eliminate the possibility for self-silence. The in-mind and out-of-body experience is internal.

Rule 4: Embrace silence. This isn't just the absence of noise, but rather the willingness to let your mind be undirected—to let it flow. Don't go with the flow—be the flow.

Rule 5: Be alone. Use the time on the chairlift to prepare your mind, or as you reach toward the wilderness, to empty yourself of all thoughts beyond the strides you are taking. If there is someone there to talk to you, it isn't going to happen.

Rule 6: Be prepared. This means not just being in shape for the activity and being expert enough to handle whatever terrain you are on, but being mystically balanced in such a way that you are prepared for the unexpected. How can you be prepared for the unexpected? It is a point called the pivot of the Tao, where the mind is devoid of thoughts. If that inner radiance arrives, you will know it.

Rule 7: Do not seek to understand. If we could understand the ephemeral, perhaps we could put it into words. We can do neither.

Rule 8: Feel the source of power and use it. Where it comes from is unimportant.

Another word for aerobic meditation might be dance. In the language of the Omaha Tribe, the words for dance and love are the same.

One of the great advocates for saving the planet and embracing nature was Dolores LaChapelle (1926-2007). Born of Native American heritage and a lifelong advocate for "deep ecology," she was a mountain climber, scientific investigator, ski instructor, Tai Chi enthusiast, writer, and exemplary citizen. She described deep ecology as upholding the rights of every form of life, both human and nonhuman, and promoting diversity, symbiosis, local economy, and decentralization. Much of the information here comes from an interview she gave to Jonathan White included in his book Talking on the Water.

She describes a day skiing at Alta, Utah, when it was snowing graupel—hard, round, marble-sized pellets that sting your face and roll down the snow. Sane skiers were in the lodge, but Dolores and five others braved the torture of the chair rides for the bliss of the trip through the trees, the only place they could see enough to ski. The six of them floated effortlessly down the mountain, never thinking of colliding with a tree or each other; never wondering where to turn or how to maneuver. It was as precisely unordered as a flock of geese taking off wing to wing and never touching, never losing formation. It was seamless, without thought or direction. She likened it to Bach's saying he did not play music; the music played him.

The experience was sacred. It contained an essential connectedness to the mountain. In the deep powder, she explained, if you try to force a turn, you fall. In Taoist thinking it is called Wu Wei, which is not "doing nothing" but "refraining from activity contrary to nature." After all, skiing is essentially a modestly controlled fall, and the less control, the less effort, the better the result. In three feet of powder, there are no landmarks for your feet, there is no bottom, it's just you and gravity. No wonder it is sublime.

She says that you cannot think your way into nature; you have to experience it and know that you are part of it with no questions asked. She favors rituals, especially those that were traditionally celebrated around the harvest and the hunt or the changing of seasons. Such festivals include all living things and embrace myth, art, dance, games, and sex, all of which connect us with our unconscious. The festivals have to be real and spontaneous. If they are contrived, they are divisive.

Gertrude Stein, famous for her questions, asked: "Is it better to be scared than to be bored?" Dolores LaChapelle was never bored. She said, "Powder skiing is not fun. It's life, fully lived—life lived in a blaze of reality." This from a woman who survived being tossed by an avalanche.

CHAPTER 26

Peak Experiences

The higher you get, the higher you get.

—IDAHO SKI HUT

Abraham Maslow defines a peak experience as a transcendent episode in which we can see our life in absolute perspective. Mountain climber Anatoli Boukreev describes summiting an 8,000-meter mountain as being reborn—being alone with your soul. Elite athletes in all sports wonder at how they exceeded personal limitations, how they found another gear, a lung full of air when there was none to be had, got up when they thought they couldn't. The experience is described as thrilling, scary, sublime, ephemeral; but in truth it is a nonconceptual experience—something that thought cannot translate.

The question here is how many of these can we have? How many Saul-on-the-road-to-Damascus—Kaboom! It's God calling—experiences does life hold, and can we make a steady diet of them? Answer is no. A life of all peak experiences would bleach the term of meaning. It would become pedestrian and boring and probably would kill us in the bargain.

Here is an analogy from my days as a naval engineering officer. Steam propulsion ships (that is, postsail and prenuclear) use oil-fired boilers to heat water and produce steam that flows through and turns the blades of turbines. But the turbines turn far too fast to attach directly to a propeller shaft. So massive reduction gears slow the speed to a manageable level and are connected to the shafts and the propellers that make the ship go. Our minds act like reduction gears to filter and organize the high-speed onslaught of information and stimulation that comes our way on a constant basis. We trust our minds to do this so we are not overwhelmed. We cannot live at a peak pace.

There are plenty of other emotions on the shelf, like love of various flavors, sorrow, frustration, elation, surprise, loneliness, happiness, contentment, reverence, sadness, peace, fright, depression, gratefulness, and the list goes on. Walt Whitman in his Songs of the Open Road speaks repeatedly of nature as the source of happiness:

> *The efflux of the soul is happiness, here is happiness.*
> *I think it pervades the open air, waiting at all times.*
> *Now it flows into us, we are rightly changed.*

Plato's dialogue "Phaedrus" is about love, and keeping in mind that Socrates was not above throwing out suckerballs to mislead those not prepared to think for themselves, he lists four kinds of madness that are beneficial to humans: prophecies from Delphi that give guidance to cities and individuals; madness that consoles, like prayers or mystic rights; madness from the muses, like poetry, music, and wine; and, finally, love, which he calls divine madness.

His metaphor for the soul is the divine chariot with two winged horses and a charioteer. This chariot can deliver the rider to the mountain where truth and reality are present, but only the gods can experience this. The most noble of humans, whom he declares to be the philosophers—no surprise there—can come close and get an obstructed view. For the rest, the chariot has a white (good) horse on the right and a dark (bad) horse on the left. The good horse seeks for the human to have a perfect love with a beautiful boy (whoops, sounding a lot like pedophilia here and with good reason). The dark horse just wants to jump on the boy and possess him without love, honor, modesty, or self-control. The charioteer jerks on the reins, the chariot descends to earth, the horses' wings disappear, and humanity is left with the joy and pain of love mixed together.

Plato is proclaimed, by a not so scientific polling of professional philosophers, to be one of the five greatest in Western philosophy, but I confess that the above dialogue leaves me entirely without substance. At the end Socrates declares that intellectual love is best, but the whole business about the bifurcated nature of humankind is much better described by the ego, id, and superego of Freud. The Greek proclivity for man-boy love is, in our culture, a felony, and good intention or nobility is not a defense. Wittgenstein, who is also considered one of the five greatest, thought reading Plato's dialogues a "frightful waste of time." I feel the same way about Wittgenstein, but fortunately, he didn't write much.

Not far down the mountainside from peak experiences is happiness. This is a pursuit, as Jefferson tells us in the Declaration of Independence, and it is the sole purpose of ethics, according to Aristotle. In much of our modern electronic communications, however, the pursuit of happiness has evolved into a contest where—by my next tweet, my next photo of my exquisite meal, my next selfie beside a celebrity—I try to convince you that I am happier, my life is more interesting, and I am having more fun than you. I know that is not most people's intent, but it is the result. Happiness should not be a zero-sum game where mine necessarily excludes or diminishes yours. In fact, happiness should expand exponentially the more it is shared and the more who are included.

Happiness cannot be our only emotion any more than we can feast upon a steady diet of peak experiences. At Passover, Jews drop some wine to remember sorrows before drinking to happiness. Life contains a full range of emotions, and it is unhealthy at best to pretend one is always happy, always on top of the world, never troubled, never blue. Neal Gladstone, a wonderful purveyor and performer of songs, has written one for single women bemoaning the lack of attractive men. The lyrics, as sung by Barbara Gladstone and Audrey Perkins, advise: "Just lower your standards, lower your standards / …And like a fungus, he will grow on you / …Though he may not be too smart, still he's got all the right parts / So lower your standards, he's just a man."

Humorist Kin Hubbard quips that it is pretty hard to know what brings happiness. Poverty and wealth have both failed.

Next question is whether the idea of love is more compelling than love itself. A popular writer made this assertion in a book, and when I, as the moderator at a public reading, asked him to elaborate, he would only say, "That's what I wrote." What a jerk. I guess another way to put the question is: "Is fantasy better than reality?"

There is plenty of fantasy with the word love attached, and most of it is totally vacuous. Love, in my experience, is giddy for a while, comfortable for a while, and constantly in need of attention just like a garden. It can wilt and die without attention, or it can prosper and grow. It can, as the lyrics of many a country song proclaim, just wander away like a maverick calf.

There is, beyond the flaming beginning, a maturing and evolving that is beautiful and rewarding, but there is no one size fits all love relationship. I suspect they all have certain characteristics such as mutual respect, communication, a certain amount of selflessness, and sex, but the recipe is written by the lovers. The Old Testament word for sexual relations is "knowing." It is the right word because it is totally ambiguous.

Snow-Bound: A Winter Idyl

JOHN GREENLEAF WHITTIER (1807-1892)

The sun that brief December day
Rose cheerless over hills of gray,
And, darkly circled, gave at noon
A sadder light than waning moon.
Slow tracing down the thickening sky
Its mute and ominous prophecy,
A portent seeming less than threat,
It sank from sight before it set.
A chill no coat, however stout,
Of homespun stuff could quite shut out,
A hard, dull bitterness of cold,
That checked, mid-vein, the circling race
Of life-blood in the sharpened face,
The coming of the snow-storm told.
The wind blew east; we heard the roar
Of Ocean on his wintry shore,
And felt the strong pulse throbbing there
Beat with low rhythm our inland air.

. . . .

So all night long the storm roared on:
The morning broke without a sun;
In tiny spherule traced with lines
Of Nature's geometric signs,
In starry flake, and pellicle,
All day the hoary meteor fell;

And, when the second morning shone,
We looked upon a world unknown,
On nothing we could call our own.
Around the glistening wonder bent
The blue walls of the firmament,
No cloud above, no earth below,—
A universe of sky and snow!

. . . .

CHAPTER 27

Jonathan Chaffee

The temptation to quit will be greatest just before you are about to succeed.

—CHINESE PROVERB

A uthor's note: Jonathan Chaffee was an Olympic biathlete, described by teammate Jay Bowerman as having "an incredible motor." He earned a PhD from Harvard in cell biology but chose to spend a career as a developer of low-income and cooperative housing, a champion of programs for the food insecure, and an advocate for energy-efficient retrofits. His selfless efforts define him, in the most honorific sense, as a citizen. I asked him to reflect on his life on the snow.

A great deal of endurance athletics takes place in the mind. There's technique; what you have practiced and learned to do is in the first instance in the mind—what you are telling yourself to do. It is an impediment until it moves from the cortex (the conscious) to the cerebellum (unconscious). Of course, if it is wrong, it's still wrong if ingrained.

I have to stop myself from accosting inexperienced skiers awkwardly skating, body twisted to the side with one foot and both arms stuck up in the air. "Don't think about picking your foot up," I want to yell. "Think about stepping onto that foot." Or seeing someone who has used the Nordic Trac apparatus, skiing classic by pushing one foot back while dividing their weight between front and back skis. "No, no," I want to say. "It's like socks on the gym floor. Jump completely onto the forward foot and glide."

I myself never had any ski coaching to speak of. My high school coach had been a jumper. My college coach was an Alpine skier. I went to the Biathlon Center, where the coach—Jay (Bowerman) and I would agree—was a blockheaded, just-try-harder Swede. The 1968 Olympics were my third international race.

I learned to ski after leaving the Olympics, watching a real-time Norwegian language broadcast of the fifty-kilometer race. The biathlon team had left Grenoble [the Olympic host city in France] early, and we were in the basement of the Hotel Holmenkollen in Oslo. [Harald] Grønningen, the tall Norwegian, was silhouetted in black and white skiing along a ridge across the screen. "I see what they are doing!" I yelled. His pole and his knee thrust forward in perfect synchrony with the opposite leg kick. Then the other side in synchrony. Bam…(pause)…Bam. In contrast, I had trained myself to kick very strongly, but swing my arm forward the smallest fraction of a second later, in a broken rhythm like walking; Oom-Pah, my head bobbing.

As a teammate and I skied in local races in Sweden, I watched the other racers carefully. Then when the team returned to Alaska, I isolated myself and skied fifty kilometers a day, for two weeks until I got the hang of it. Not only could I do it, I was full of it and would gladly explain it to anyone who would listen. Jay, working on this himself, was the only one interested.

I went back to college that fall, and my ski training consisted of running up the stairwell of a seventeen-story building on campus. I skied in local races in Vermont and New Hampshire and was very fast. At a local club race, I was accused of having cut off a portion because "the guys" couldn't believe my time. I never could beat Bob Gray or Mike Gallagher, but, in a short ten-kilometer race I could beat pretty much anyone else. I felt invincible.

I was chosen for the 1970 FIS [international ski governing board] team and had the good fortune to experience skiing in the Holmenkollen King's Cup, with 50,000 spectators pressed into the snow fence yelling encouragement, calling out my splits to me. I started two minutes ahead of a Norwegian A-team member, and he did not catch me. Teammates watching said later that they could hear me coming, gasping for air, before they saw me. I had a good race. "Maybe I broke into it," I thought. In fact, I was the second US skier. Gallagher was twenty-sixth, and I was over fiftieth place. That was where I really stood in world competition, and no amount of training was going to change it very much. Although I was good compared to US skiers, and I was in outstanding condition, I was not as good as dozens of Norwegians, lots of Swedes, Finns, Russians and Italians. We US skiers used to say that while our conditioning was excellent (I'm sure I could have beaten many of those skiers in a footrace up a mountain), we had mostly begun skiing in high school and didn't have the early years of experience to allow us to ski fast effortlessly. And, realistically, I never accrued the kilometers and hours of skiing that are the norm at the World Cup level. I was always an amateur, and except for a year and one half at the Biathlon Center, I trained only about seven or eight hours a week; while serious international competitors train at least twice that.

Out today with a friend at the Dartmouth College cross-country venue, we were passed by a skier with a beautiful technique, hips thrusting forward at every stride. My friend hurried ahead to engage him. He was Norwegian and had been on the Norwegian national team in the early 1990s. As he skied away my friend (himself a phenomenal skier, the best in his generation, who in his sixties could still beat Dartmouth ski team members, but whose technique is not beautiful) enthused: "Look at how smooth he is. I could tell he was Norwegian. Look at him."

One could imagine that technique would not matter that much in an endurance sport, but in fact, at the highest levels of the sport, good technique is "that without which." I can still coach myself to ski well, with good form, for a short time, but good technique is being able to ski fast, fluidly, for a long time. Good technique cannot be consciously maintained, but has to be committed as a complex and varying sequence to unconscious muscle memory by long hours of practice, so that it doesn't take effort to maintain the technique itself. Obviously, there is some component of trying harder, as we see athletes putting out peak performances at their home venues, but it can only enhance, not replace, good technique.

Trying harder can be the enemy of good technique by using too much effort early in the race. Watching World

Cup races on YouTube, I sometimes see an American skier near the front in the first half of the race, ahead of the winners, who are biding their time back in the pack.

After leaving the biathlon team, I had returned to Cambridge and was training hard, but for a maximum of one hour. So my liver and muscles stored only an hour's worth of glycogen. A couple of times, training longer hours with the national team, I learned the consequences of running out of fuel for carbohydrate metabolism. The academic term is "bonking." The first time was during a training camp at Dartmouth. A race was scheduled from the Ravine Lodge at the bottom of Mount Moosilauke to the top. The trail at that time went straight up, and it took only about 30 minutes, so the guys said, "Let's go back another way to get a workout." I had no idea where we were, except that we ran on and on. My hands began to tingle, and my vision narrowed to a tunnel. "Be careful," I mumbled to myself. "Don't stumble." Alone, I couldn't go on and collapsed in a sunny spot, my head down a bank. Legendary coach Al Merrill came along. "How're ya doing, Tiger?" he asked and kept going. After a while Charlie Kellogg appeared. I had trained with him in Cambridge, and he was in the same condition. "I know where we are," he said. "We're only about a half mile from the lodge, and it's all flat. What kind of men are we? Let's get up and go." So we got up and went, about two steps, leaning on each other, before sitting down again. We were still sitting, marveling that we couldn't make ourselves move, when Charlie's wife, Jill, came back along the trail bringing orange slices and cookies, just enough to enable us to get to the lodge. Still buzzing, I looked around desperately for something to eat and found a small tin of maple syrup on a window sill. Upending it, the sugar shot down my arms like fire. I ran up the steps to the waiting vans, completely recovered.

It happened again on a bike ride in the Putney area with Bob Gray and some prospective Olympians, including Martha Rockwell. I asked how long we intended to ride, and Bob said we'd go over to Newfane, and then we would see. We biked for hours through picturesque Vermont towns, and when the tunnel vision and tingling hands recurred I knew what I needed. Turning down a driveway, I dropped my bike on the lawn and stumbled across the porch to the front door, my cleats clack clacking. "Don't slur your words," I cautioned myself, "or they will be afraid." I asked for water (in those days we didn't carry water bottles, nor anything to eat; feeding stations were offered during races, but it wasn't part of training), and they invited me in. Clack-clack cleats. As they filled the glass at the kitchen sink, I saw a sugar bowl on the table. "Do you mind?" I scooped spoonfuls into the water and gulped it down. Immediately recovered, I explained what had happened to me. "Oh yes," they laughed. "We know Bob Gray." The others were waiting at the next intersection, and acknowledged that we were still a long way from home and that they were getting hungry too. We passed a large lawn party in a yard alongside and above the road, separated by a fence. Bob stopped us. "No, no we can't do that," we said. "We're all sweaty." "It's OK," Bob said. "I know the people who live here and their kids that got married." So wearing our tiny biking shorts amid the wedding finery, we filed down the food line, trying not to be seen eating with our fingers.

Which brings me to the other side of the technique coin: exultation. This is what the metaphysics of endurance athletics makes me think of. There are times when the normal laws of physics, that movement requires input of energy, don't seem to apply, when it seems that the mental image of your movement carries you by itself. You live for those times, but even the best athletes cannot completely control getting into that state, leading to lots of superstition. It is easy, and common, to train harder to seek this "state" and then kill it completely with overtraining.

One can labor and despair and then somehow transcend effort. I had such an experience in the Craftsbury Marathon in the old days where the competitors were bused out to a resort and skied fifty kilometers through farms and fields and woods to finish in the town green of Craftsbury. I went out too fast and tired myself out on the big initial uphill. Three younger racers caught me, and I jumped in behind them, at first struggling to keep up, then settling into the pace. We ate up the kilometers. When the leader switched tracks, we all switched. When the leader tucked, we all tucked. When the leader stood up and checked before a turn, we all followed suit. It was exhilarating.

A little beyond the halfway mark, I began to feel the pace was lagging. We came down a steep hill into a sharp uphill, and I stepped into the other track and exploded, double polling up the hill by my friends. Thirty minutes later, I regretted my move as my energy sagged. Another racer caught me and pulled me from forty to forty-nine kilometers. Climbing the long corn field into Craftsbury, I regained my joy and turned to my friend. "Shall we go for it from here?" Then I double polled like a maniac to the finish. It was one of the most fun races I have had.

There was another phenomenon I experienced that was metaphysical. Time slowed to a standstill. The Steward Mountain Marathon is from Main Street at sea level up a 3,000-foot mountain and back down. We practiced for this by running up and down very steep hills. The trail went about halfway up the mountain on dirt through the woods before emerging onto a ridge of shale-like rock. From the top, the initial descent was down a gully filled with loose scree, which I ran in great striding leaps. Then the down trail crossed the up trail and went down a brook bed, over rocks. I thought, "What if my foot slips? I could break my leg." And then, "No, if my foot slips, I will just lift it up and place it on another rock. There is plenty of time. My body has enough forward momentum that it will not drop. My feet can move independently beneath it." The sensation of my body floating while my legs could move independently from my weight carried over into my skiing. Time slowed way down, as it does in an accident. I could accelerate at will.

Endurance movement seems to be borne by the mental image, but it is not a normal mental process that assesses and reassesses the physical cost of moving. It is more like an out-of-body mental state in which the physical cost is not to be counted. It is an extended gesture; an exultation.

CHAPTER 28

Sawtooth Mountain Guides and Kirk Bachman

The only faint source of hope
is the snow on Kurakake Mountain.

—GARY SNYDER, poet

"Snow is a super-dynamic medium—how it forms in the atmosphere and how it changes once on the ground is fascinating to observe—much like a time lapse of geology on steroids." So says Kirk Bachman, and after a lifetime on and around the snow, and as the founder of Sawtooth Mountain Guides in Stanley, Idaho, some thirty-five years ago, he should know. He has spent a career getting people out into the wilderness. (He doesn't just take them there; he brings them back, too).

Sun and wind and temperature give nuance to snow, and the changes it makes are observable, if you pay attention. The variations, the multiple personalities of snow, are why people get such vitality out of it. As snow changes, it is a microcosm that depicts life. To be tuned into it is a gift from nature. Kirk's life as a mountain guide is dedicated to sharing the privilege of living with nature, and yet nature remains, in the best Taoist sense, "the unanswerable answer."

A sense of place is the key to being an authentic wilderness guide according to Kirk. "Watching the clouds play with the sun and the mountain, you feel connected to this place. It is home. It becomes part of who you are; you have a rapport with the land, and you share what you know about it. A lot of this sharing is unspoken."

His clients become his friends as the wilderness plays a particular role in binding people to each other. The people he is guiding range from those who are seeking adventure but do not have the acumen to do it on their own to hardened backcountry types who want the challenge of a particular steep couloir to ski, a dynamic route through the backcountry, or the guide's unique knowledge of where the best powder, untouched by sun or wind, lies.

There is an element of danger inherent in the backcountry. That is part of the attraction, but a mis-adventure is not. The guide's job is to be an intermediary who teaches how to read the snow, avoid avalanches, and deal with the weather when it turns nasty. Seasoned guides are good with people, matching interests and abilities and respecting limitations. They have an authenticity born of respect for the spectacular and unforgiving force of nature. No greeting card sentiment here; nature delivers real, life-adjusting lessons.

Snowflakes are made up of crystals that vary in shape. Some are six-sided prisms while others are stellar plates with six arms that form a hexagon. Flakes can be shaped like needles that are long and flat, but in colder temperatures become three-dimensional. Stellared dendrites or stellared ferns look like little Christmas trees and are the stuff of powder snow. The graupel that Dolores LaChapelle described in "Chapter 25" are rounded, marble-like snowflakes that have fallen through supercooled droplets that are below freezing but remain liquid. There is lots to learn about snow.

Winter guides teach their companions about avalanches, where the mountain holds unstable snow, how to track the snowpack's seasonal changes, and how to test its layers. Anticipating dangers and making good decisions for tour planning are critical skills, along with practice for rescues should the unexpected require a group to respond.

Kirk is also a yurt builder, a skill he first acquired as a student at Idaho State University. To prepare for a move to the central Idaho mountains, he constructed his first yurt as his residence. He connected up with Joe Leonard, the legendary personality of the Sawtooths (See Chapter 14). Joe had built a few rudimentary log structures, and Kirk's yurts intrigued him because they were more comfortable, more efficient, and more acceptable to the Forest Service, which discouraged permanent structures on government land. The yurt harks back to the days of Genghis Khan and the nomads of the Mongolian steppes. Kirk makes the roof beams from standing dead lodgepole pines, preparing the poles with a draw knife, and then pairing them with the latticework sides, cover skin, and various fittings that hold the whole structure together. The beauty of the yurt design is that it can be packed up and moved, which is what the original inhabitants of yurts did as they followed their herds seasonally.

Kirk's fascinating Sawtooth Outback website (www.saw-toothoutback.com) describes summer and winter outdoor wilderness adventures. What makes it so fitting to Kirk's personality (he combined a study of philosophy and the environment in college) is the breadth of topics it embraces. His web domain is "where I have been on the trail" and includes friends he has made whose work he particularly appreciates. Beat poet and Zen aficionado Gary Snyder, along with artist and sculptor Rusty Bowman, whose creations use Native American techniques and materials from the land, such as red and yellow ochre pigments, beeswax, moose ligaments, and willow twig hair are linked.

Also featured are the exquisite instruments of luthiers Lawrence Smart and Austin Clark, makers of mandolins, guitars, and octave mandolins (mandolin configuration, but the size of a small guitar). The videos and stills of mountain adventures around the world make one want to get out there and commune.

While the popularity of Alpine skiing may have peaked, backcountry touring has prospered with the development of all-terrain gear, such as bindings with a loose heal for climbing that can lock down on the descent. Such improvements have made the backcountry more accessible to competent Alpine skiers, and overnighting in one of Kirk's yurts means more time to do the fun stuff.

There is a fascination in trusting one's passion for life to nature. Nature abides as a foundation for life, but unlike the city, where predictability is the norm, nature will give you what she wants, and if your eyes and ears are open to her, she will fill your heart. Yes, you can bite off more than you can chew sometimes, but that is when you want to have a Sawtooth Mountain Guide with you to collect the pieces. You will never feel more alive.

For Kirk, it is an ongoing adventure. He is passionate about "giving people the keys to the castle" by sharing what he knows from a lifetime of gathering experiences and weaving them together. He reminds himself that "as one gets older, it is important to put guardrails on your thinking about the hazards of nature." But while what's slowing down for Kirk might seem fast to many of us, he says he still watches where he puts his feet.

CHAPTER 29

Risk and Reward

All religions, all teachings, are synthesized
in the Himalayas.

—NICHOLAS ROERICH, Russian artist and philosopher

Hilaree Nelson and Jim Morrison climbed Lhotse—at 27,940 feet, the fourth-highest mountain on earth—and skied down its face. Why would anyone want to do that? Anything above 24,000 feet (approximately 8,000 meters) is known as the death zone, where the body literally is consuming itself and one cannot eat or sleep or recover from the inhuman exertion it takes to climb.

Both speak about their undertaking in the film Lhotse, and they appear to be of a single mind and determination. "I tell myself it is what I love." "The mountain has helped keep me alive (after Jim's family tragedy)". "The sunrise on the summit is the why. It connects all the parts of my life so I can fully live in the now." "The danger and the suffering and the prayer flags—when you have done everything you can to set yourself up for success and the universe grants it—then you have that for the rest of your life." "It is important to take risks in life and not just wait for it to come to you. You have to take risks if you want to learn anything about yourself."

Does that do it for you? If so, you are probably already out there, maybe not linking turns together at 8,000 meters, but pushing yourself and your boundaries. If not, then maybe you are sitting in your room writing poetry like Emily Dickenson, showing herself to be one of the most courageous of human thinkers. There are lots of ways to show courage and lots of ways to find fulfilment and lots of ways to get to know yourself. What they have in common is that they usually don't come knocking, or as the old Vietnamese saying goes: "A man will stand on a hillside for a very long time before a fully roasted duck flies into his mouth."

Mount Everest is the tallest point on earth—29,029 feet—the Superbowl of climbing. Well, it would be the Superbowl if the winning team could have a bunch of extra people on the field pushing or carrying them over the goal line. That is what the Sherpas do—sometimes literally carrying the climbers up the mountain along with lugging most of their provisions, setting ropes and ladders on the most difficult portions, and sometimes dying in the process. For the Sherpas, Everest is a holy place, but the temple is overrun with worshipers and their garbage—empty oxygen cylinders, trash, abandoned tents and equipment. More than 4,000 people have summited Everest; about 600 every year at a cost of $100,000 per customer. There are so many climbing parties and so few routes and so little time for safe ascent and return that there is a literal traffic jam of climbers. It is hardly what you would call a wilderness experience, except for the fact that the conditions are as inhospitable as anywhere on earth.

It is dangerous and unpredictable. The south route, preferred by most, traverses the Khambu Icefall, a literal river of constantly moving ice chunks, some as big as a freight car, that can let loose without warning. Sherpa guides go through the icefall about thirty times a season. The Sherpas are exceptionally strong and are acclimated to the mountain and the rarity of the oxygen there. It takes a flatland climber about eight weeks to acclimatize, and while sitting around waiting for that to happen, rather than becoming more fit, the body is losing strength, hydration, and muscle tone needed for the climb. The idea is to get up and down before you die. An acquaintance from Portland wanted to do Everest, not to reach the top, but just for the experience. He was a television reporter, and he only got to about 18,000 feet before cerebral edema (swelling of the brain) killed him. The other killer edema is pulmonary, where the lungs swell so you can't breathe and you literally drown in the accumulated fluid.

The narrative of Sherpa families losing climbers goes back for generations. Bodies that aren't recovered cannot be reincarnated, according to Buddhist doctrine, thus compounding the loss. Tensing Norgay was the first Sherpa to summit Everest with Sir Edmund Hillary in 1953. Hillary would never have made it without Norgay, and yet Hillary was portrayed as the world's hero.

Russian climber Anatoli Boukreev, who accomplished twenty-one successful ascents of eleven of the world's highest peaks before he was killed in an avalanche on Annapurna on Christmas day, 1997, said: "On each journey, I am reborn.... You arrive at the top having renounced everything that you think you must have to support life and are alone with your soul. That empty vantage point lets you reappraise yourself and every relationship and object that is part of the civilized world..."

For those who succeed in reaching the summit and those who don't, the most dangerous part of the climb is on the way down. Gravity pulls you. The light may be fading or a storm approaching, and your resources of energy and slavish attention are exhausted. Your brain is starved and muddled. One misstep and...

K-2 is another of the traffic-jam mountains. In 2008, eleven people died in a single accident. The Sherpas pray to the mountain for permission to climb. Sometimes the mountain says no.

An Irish Airman Foresees His Death

WILLIAM BUTLER YEATS (1863-1939)

I know that I shall meet my fate
Somewhere among the clouds above;
Those that I fight I do not hate,
Those that I guard I do not love;
My country is Kiltartan Cross,
My countrymen Kiltartan's poor,
No likely end could bring them loss
Or leave them happier than before.
Nor law, nor duty made me fight,
Nor public men, nor cheering crowds,
A lonely impulse of delight
Drove to this tumult in the clouds;
I balanced all, brought all to mind,
The years to come seemed waste of breath,
A waste of breath the years behind
In balance with this life, this death.

CHAPTER 30

Chip Pollard and his son Eric

They sicken of the calm who know the storm.

—DOROTHY PARKER, writer

The great thing about riding the chairlift is that there is nowhere to go for about eight minutes (twenty-two minutes—a lifetime—on the old, slow chair to the top at Arizona Snowbowl near Flagstaff). If the wind is not howling too ferociously, conversations with total strangers can be delicious and enlightening.

I asked the guy on my right, whose name turned out to be Chip Pollard, what his most unusual skiing experience was. Nineteen sixty-eight. He was in the navy and was on leave skiing in Kitzbuhel, Austria. Instead of plunging right down the mountain, he decided to walk up to a knoll, catch some rays and relax. There was one other guy there, and they got to talking.

"You American?" asked Chip.

"Yep."

"Where from?"

"Boston."

"No kidding, me too. Where did you live in Boston?"

"Back Bay."

"Really, me, too."

"Yep, 39 Peterborough Street."

"You are shitting me—that is where I lived."

Turns out the guy had rented the apartment Chip had moved out of. Six degrees of separation and all that.

Not quite as coincidentally, Chip and I were in the navy at the same time, although I was in the western Pacific on a cruiser lobbing shells into the Vietnamese jungle, and he was in Europe. He was stationed on a sub-tender in Scotland and fell into a job teaching skiing and finding accommodations and equipment for American service personnel who wanted to ski there.

Chip skis beautifully, expertly, and I enjoyed a morning of following him down the mountain. Turns out he is bionic. He was still getting used to his new ankle replacement and had had a knee done—to mention just two items in his catalog of body parts that have exceeded their shelf life or been rejuvenated. Shoots the hell out of my theory that the way to keep athletically active into geezerhood is to never get out of shape and never get hurt. Actually, that theory was literally shot down several years earlier on another chair ride on the outback lift at Bachelor. I was making the same pitch to a guy about my age who allowed as how he had shot himself in the leg doing a quick draw.

As Chip and I were parting, and I was thanking him for the good company and tour of the mountain, he suggested that I check out his son Eric's video Drawn From Here. You can google it for free, and it is amazing and—because of the injuries—chilling. Taking extreme skiing to the edge means that sometimes there is a hard landing at the bottom. As the film says, "What matters is what you do next." From a fall in Russia, Eric spent fifty-four days in trauma wards there and in Germany, endured eleven surgeries, and ended up with partial paralysis in his left foot and toes. He has paid a price for adventure, no question about that, but he has produced some remarkable art, has innovated, is devoted to his family, and is roaring along in the next phase of his artistic career.

Nobody asks the question: "Is it worth it?" before actually doing it. If you ask the question, the answer is probably no, and it won't happen. After it happens, you can ask: "Was it worth it?" The answer is often ambiguous.

Some of the comments from the extreme skiers in Eric's films are "inspiration is everything"; "as soon as I begin to feel too secure about something I know I am on the wrong track"; "fear is an inner resource—it often tells you that this is exactly where you ought to go"; "to do a dangerous thing with style is what I call art"; "everything in the world conspires to crush your identity"; "making connections is what makes art, and you have to have different experiences to make creative connections." In the words of another artist, Pablo Picasso, who took lots of chances: "Learn the rules like a pro so you can break them like an artist."

On the irreverent side, as a skier jumps off the knife edge of a mountain peak to a sixty-degree slope with rocks and ice, his buddies yell, "Be safe; live 'til thirty."

Combat skiing comes at the end of the day with all the adrenaline spent. Here the skier tries to ski all the way home—along the side of the freeway, on the slightly snow-covered rocks in the stream, over the sidewalk, and down the stairway. Works great for the fearless with more than one pair of skis.

Nothing Venture Nothing Win

RUMI (1207-1273)

When you put a cargo on board a ship, you make that
venture on trust,
For you know not whether you will be drowned or come
safe to land.
If you say, "I will not embark till I am certain of my fate,"
then you will do no trade:
the secret of these two destinies is never disclosed.
The faint-hearted merchant neither gains nor loses; nay he
loses: one must take fire in order to get light.
Since all affairs turn upon hope, surely Faith is the best
object of hope, for thereby you win salvation.

Fragments

You can lie at a banquet, but you have to be
honest in the kitchen.

—WILLIAM STAFFORD, poet

I n medias res is the Latin for the literary device of starting in the middle of a story and hoping that the reader is
intrigued enough to stick with you before forcefully tossing
the book into a corner. What is going to happen in this chapter, unless the book is already airborne, is a number of poetic
fragments that bear on the topic of snow, mysticism, and the
feeling of transcendence. Poets use words more beautifully
and more precisely than any others, and it is a travesty to
take just part of a poem out of context. But these are beautiful fragments and, I hope, that beauty will excuse the insult.

A terrible beauty is born.
    —WILLIAM BUTLER YEATS, "Easter, 1916"

The best lack all conviction, while the worst
Are full of passionate intensity.
    —WILLIAM BUTLER YEATS, "The Second Coming"

Hush me, O slumbering mountains—
Send me dreams.

> —HARRIET MONROE,
> "The Blue Ridge"

Winter kept us warm, covering
Earth in forgetful snow,[…].

> —T.S. ELIOT,
> "The Wasteland"

The frolic architecture of the snow.

> —RALPH WALDO EMERSON, "
> The Snow-Storm"

Today we breathe abreast
and all the intervening decades
fade like snow.

> —SAMUEL HAZO,
> "One Day Into the World"

The task and potential greatness of mortals reside
In their ability to produce things which are at home
In everlastingness.

> —HANNAH ARENDT, "The Human Condition"

The pen is the tongue of the mind.

> —MIGUEL DE CERVANTES SAAVEDRA,
> "Don Quixote"—and yes, I know some of these quotes
> come from books not poems; cut me some slack here.

You road […] I believe you are not all that is here,
I believe that much unseen is also here.

> WALT WHITMAN,
> "Song of the Open Road

Now I see the secret of the making of the best persons,
It is to grow in the open air and to eat and sleep with
the earth.

WALT WHITMAN,
"Song of the Open Road"

From the sky in the form of snow
comes the great forgiveness.

WILLIAM STAFFORD,
"November"

And the end of our exploring
Will be to arrive where we started
And know the place for the first time.

T.S. ELIOT,
"Little Gidding"

Listen, whatever it is you try
To do with your life, nothing will ever dazzle you
Like the dreams of your body.

MARY OLIVER,
"Humpbacks"

So all night long the storm roared on:
The morning broke without a sun.

JOHN GREENLEAF WHITTIER,
"Snow-Bound: A Winter Idyl"

Oh, what a catastrophe, what a maiming of love
when it was made a personal, merely personal
feeling, taken away from the rising and the
setting of the sun, and cut off from the magic
connection of the solstice and equinox! This

is what is the matter with us. We are bleeding at the roots, because we are cut off from the earth and sun and stars, and love is a grinning mockery, because, poor blossom, we plucked it from its stem on the tree of Life, and expected it to keep on blooming in our civilized vase on the table.

D.H. LAWRENCE.
"A Propos of Lady Chatterley's Lover"

CHAPTER 32

Backcountry Learning

Adopt the pace of nature: Her secret is patience.

—RALPH WALDO EMERSON, philosopher

It is the course all of us wish we had taken in college. Scott Knickerbocker and his wife, Megan Dixon, both professors at The College of Idaho, teach an intensive four-week course every other year called Winter Wilderness Experience, where they take eight students to the Sawtooth Valley in Stanley, Idaho, to live, write, and backcountry ski. Scott's expertise is in American literature, and Megan's is in cultural geography. Together the students and professors closely read fine writing about outdoor experiences such as Ernest Hemingway's short story "Cross-Country Snow" and Jack London's "To Build a Fire." Students write in their journals daily. They learn to telemark ski and read the snow for signs of potential avalanche. They develop the eyes to identify trees, and plants, and peaks around them, and the ears to hear the snow if it whumps and settles or the birds that can rough it there for the winter and chirp or squawk about it.

The students come away from the month's experience

"in a different place"; a place that will permanently enrich their lives.

A sense of place is at the heart of the course. Place is both a point on a map and a point of view. It is an appreciation of what that location contains and a place in our minds that catalogs, examines, and appreciates it. It is seeing what is there and seeing with new eyes. It is intense concentration to one's surroundings and the ability to let those surroundings flow in such a way that we know, feel, and experience what is not there. It is like Hemingway's idea that the excellence of writing can be judged by the excellence of what is written and then left out. On a less reverent note, however, writer Ray Bradbury (Fahrenheit 491) said: "I've written thousands of words that no one will ever see. I had to write them to get rid of them."

The real stuff of education, indeed of genius, is making connections. This interdisciplinary course erases the artificial boundaries that college education imposes, and it allows the students, as they write in their journals, to see that close reading of a text and close reading of nature—the smell of the pines, for example—are related. Much of our technological environment allows us to pay only "partial attention," and as Scott points out, in the wilderness, partial attention can get you killed.

Jack London's "To Build a Fire" is such a cautionary tale. Ecological ignorance has its consequences. The protagonist of the story, who is called only "the man," is not able to imagine. "He was not much of a thinker," London tells us. So he undertakes a daylong trek in the Yukon after being warned not to go out in sub-fifty-below cold. It is actually 107 degrees below freezing. Nature is ominous and unforgiving from the opening sentence, a clear reference to the unformed earth in the second verse of Genesis: "…there seemed to be an indescribable darkness over the face of things…" The day goes on; the cold is relentless. "[His] blood was alive, like the dog. Like the dog, it wanted to hide and seek cover, away from the fearful cold." The dog, part wolf, survives; the man does not. Nature always has the last word.

Mornings in the cabin, the students read—that is, really read—the texts and discuss them, but much of the instruction is on the treks. While students come in with different athletic experience and abilities, telemarking is "a bit of a leveler," and many find they can do things with their bodies they hadn't before experienced.

In backcountry skiing, there are no lifts, and the strength you develop in the 90 percent of the time you are climbing sustains you for the exhilarating swoosh down through the trees. They learn to observe the snow, how it lies, and by digging to see how it is layered. They read Hemingway about tourists who shame an experienced guide into taking them out when the snow is unstable (they die in an avalanche). Mental breakthroughs and physical exertion are helpmates. Likewise, careful evaluation of dangers, of group dynamics, and of the tremendous value of deliberately scaring yourself are part of the curriculum. It is the sublime and energizing function of nature to give us power and keep us in our place.

CHAPTER 33

Freedom

> I think of a hero as someone who
> understands the degree of responsibility
> that comes with his freedom.
>
> —BOB DYLAN, musician

This is a big topic. There are many kinds of freedom: physical, intellectual, societal, religious, instinctual, musical, artistic, spiritual—just to name a few. Franklin Delano Roosevelt's four freedoms, articulated in his State of the Union speech in 1941, were freedom of speech and worship and freedom from want and fear. Two freedoms of and two freedoms from.

The five freedoms of the First Amendment are: religion, speech, press, assembly, and petition. What follows is the text of the First Amendment—sorry, I can't help it. It is the single most important part of our democracy, and we won't keep it if we don't protect it:

Congress shall make no law respecting an establishment of religion, or prohibiting the free exercise thereof; or abridging the freedom of speech, or of the press, or of the right of the people peaceably to assemble, and to petition the Government for a redress of grievances.

What this means is that no public official, low or mighty, can tell you what to think, what to believe or how to seek information. No official can prevent you from choosing your own friends and allies or from telling the government why you think it is misbehaving. It is, at least in theory, how we avoid violent revolution. It is how we are supposed to listen to each other. And believe me, this is not a political statement; it is a raw plea to right the ship: injecting religion into politics, calling criticism "fake news," and vilifying the press are a frontal attack on our democracy. We shouldn't stand for it.

Okay. Got that off my chest. Now back to the mountain. Freedom—physical freedom—is, from my interviews of skiers of all abilities, the primary reason they love the sport. It is the freedom from gravity as you zip down the mountain (my friend Andy's phone said he went 63.5 miles per hour today). It is why skiers and boarders launch themselves off jumps. It is true of the most raw novice because he or she can go so much faster on the snow than any human can go on feet and dry land. What it proves, I think, is that what we really appreciate about life is always just outside of our comfort zone. That reach is the boundary between the commonplace and the mystical.

A lifelong backcountry skier, reflecting on his first experience, said that the pillowy snow and the trees and the quiet erased everything else from his mind. Nothing else mattered. It is that hoovering up of all of the detritus in our heads that clears the way for inspiration. As psychoanalyst Carl Jung wrote in "Memories, Dreams, Reflections":

> The more the critical reason dominates, the more impoverished life becomes; but the more of the unconscious, and the more of myth we are capable of making conscious, the more of life we integrate.

This kind of expanding consciousness, of accommodating one's self to an unseen order, is consistent with the tradition of weyekin. Weyekin is the Nez Perce word for a kind of spiritual being or spirit guide. Everything—rocks, trees, birds—has a spirit, and the weyekin can be a mediator to this unseen universe. After tutoring from an elder, young people, ages twelve to fifteen, go out into the wilderness without food, without shelter or fire, fasting and seeking. The most receptive will be visited by their weyekin, sometimes in the form of an animal or bird, who will, for a lifetime, aid them in their hunts, crops, relationships. The Nez Perce look at the land as a gift and believe that if people take care of the water, fish, game, roots and spirits, the earth will take care of them.

Ursula Le Guin, an extraordinarily original thinker and writer, said that some of the California Indians knew that the name of an animal was a metaphysical event that would bring the spirit of that animal along with it. The hunt, the hunter, the deer, and the "deerness" were part of the unified and mystical world, and the hunter would look to the gift of the deerness for the success of the hunt. "When we name something, we are naming its essence, and therefore its sacredness."

Le Guin says that in our modern "civilization" we may know a lot, but we have had to give up a lot to know what we know. The mystical, which is indescribable in words, has to be one of these.

Creative freedom demands a letting go, much like letting go of the temptation to turn your skis uphill into the mountain, and instead pointing them down the fall-line and letting out a primal scream. This is abandonment. This is cutting loose the self-restraints. This is letting your body do what it is trained to do and leaving your mind, for the time being, at home. But training is crucial for freedom. "You've got to practice, practice, practice. And then, when you finally get up there on the bandstand, forget all that and just wail," said jazz great Charlie Parker.

Letting one's mind play is often the very best way to solve problems. We have an ever-active mind that is working away while the rest of us is elsewhere. We also can change our minds. That is a kind of freedom and, according to Einstein, a measure of intelligence. And to keep freedom, we have to protect freedom, especially the freedom to speak of those with whom we disagree. It is counterintuitive, I know, but once I prevent you from speaking, there is no protection for me. And besides, perhaps by encouraging you to speak, you will prove to the world that you are a fool. This, of course, could not possibly happen to me.

Ordeal

NINA CASSIAN (1924-2014)
TRANSLATED FROM ROMANIAN BY MICHAEL
IMPEY AND BRIAN SWANN

I promise to make you more alive than you've ever been.
For the first time you'll see your pores opening
like the gills of a fish and you'll hear
the noise of blood in galleries
and feel light gliding on your corneas
like the dragging of a dress across the floor.
For the first time, you'll note gravity's prick
like a thorn in your heel,
and your shoulder blades will hurt from the imperative of
wings.
I promise to make you so alive that
the fall of dust on furniture will deafen you,
and you'll feel your eyebrows like two wounds forming
and your memories will seem to begin
with the creation of the world.

CHAPTER 34

Tubby

Courage is rightly deemed the first of human
qualities...it is the quality that guarantees all others.

—WINSTON CHURCHILL, British prime minister

Tubby Clayton was vicar of London's All Hallows by the
Tower and vicar to the queen. He was also the founder
of Toc H, the British Empire service organization, and he
was a chaplain to British troops during the Great War when
the "Bosch" (Germans) were shooting artillery over the Old
House in Ypres, Belgium, and hitting their own troops on
the other side. (The Old House—Talbot House—was just a
house then; it subsequently became something of a shrine).
Early in World War II, this same Tubby—a name not inap-
propriate to his physical stature—learned that British oil
tankers were regularly being torpedoed but lacked on-board
chaplains. So, he volunteered, a man then in his fifties.

I got to know Tubby as a Winant Volunteer in the
summer of 1962. The Winant Volunteers were a bunch of
energetic, well-meaning and pretty much clueless American college students who worked in English youth clubs
and other social services for a summer. My placement was

in Bristol, and we taught basketball, played soccer as if it were American football, went camping in the rain in Wales, sang songs, and generally had a good time. Although World War II had been over for more than fifteen years, it was still very much on the minds and in the psyches of our leaders. At the end of the summer, I was invited to go to the Old House with Tubby and some others to talk about the next year, when I was supposed to return as his aide. I learned to eat blackened peas (the English vets who pretended to cook, couldn't), drink tea with milk, and relive with them the horrors, and, I am sorry to say, the glories of war.

This is all prologue to the closest I have ever come to a mystical or religious experience. The Upper Room in the Old House at Ypres was the chapel, and I was up there one night kneeling and decided I would just stay that way until something happened. I waited and sort of went into a trancelike state; and Tubby said, "Let me give you a blessing," put his hand on my head, and said a prayer. My skin crawled. My flesh felt hot. That was it. It didn't last long, but it was… It was what? I was not a changed person. Not born again. Not transformed in any way, except to have felt something I knew was not ordinary.

The next morning I was to catch an early bus to meet some friends and tour around Europe, so I said goodbye to Tubby and promised to correspond with verses from Pilgrim's Progress (which he knew by heart, and I knew not at all). I got up with my monster suitcase and was standing out in the road waiting for the bus, and there comes Tubby waddling along in his pajamas and bathrobe with the blood red sun coming up behind him as he muttered some poetry about the old and young and rebirth. The bus came, and that was it. But it is annealed on my memory as if it happened yesterday.

I saw him again the next year when he was touring the United States and came to Stanford with the strangest assortment of briefcases (about five of them), each holding some collection of important papers suitable for functions known only to him. I got him a footlocker trunk to hold them all along with a bottle of sherry, which he managed to consume forthwith, and off he went. I didn't see him again but remember him with greatest affection. He was a man of faith and courage.

He was also a caricature of himself. At the Old House, before dinner, a bunch of us were gathered in the kitchen to watch the ritual slaughter of the food by the gunnery sergeant. One of us sat on the edge of the table on which the crockery was stacked, the table gave way, with the whole lot hitting the floor in pieces. Silence. At last Tubby said, "Now then"—which is what he always said.

I guess you had to be there.

CHAPTER 35

The Senses

For the poet is light, winged, and holy. There is no
invention in him until he has been inspired, out of
his senses, and has no mind.

—SOCRATES TO ION

S ee, that is what I have been trying to say all along—and
it was said, definitively, over 2,500 years ago. What is
mystical is best said by the poets, and what the poets say
is dependent on something beyond normal experience
("somewhere i have never travelled, gladly beyond / any
experience[…]," wrote e.e.cummings). So the walk-about
in this chapter is of the senses and the poets. And the mind.

Let's start with Howard Gardner and his study of the multiple intelligences: Frames of Mind, published first in 1983
and again in 1993. Seemingly forever in educational theory,
intelligence was measured by reading, writing and 'rithme-
tic—think the McGuffey Reader. Gardner's research told him
that people are differently abled, and intelligence is much
broader, including such abilities as music, personal relations,
and spatial relationships. Several of these are particularly
important for skiing, namely spatial and bodily-kinesthetic.

Music helps, too, particularly in the rhythm department.

If you are spatially abled, you can see things in dimensions; you know how things go together; you can picture them in your mind. When you can picture the slope in your mind and rotate the turns and undulations you are less likely to be surprised and thrown back on your skis when going fast. It was said of the Stanford Cardinal and then Indianapolis Colts quarterback Andrew Luck that his training in architecture enhanced his spatial skills in seeing the whole playing field and its rapidly changing dimensions. Sculptors and painters have this intelligence—at least the good ones do. Visualization concentrates the mental energy in preparation for the physical.

Bodily-kinesthetic ability is the most obvious aid to skiers and boarders, but until Gardner came along, not many called it intelligence. Since the days when Plato was translating the insights of Socrates, the mind has been thought to be superior to the body. Descartes penned the most famous phrase in philosophy: cogito ergo sum—I think, therefore I am. But the body does some pretty great stuff. It can leap and crouch and change directions, and shift weight and flex and bend, all with precision and timing. It can train itself to do all of these things on command, and with fluidity and grace and sequence. It can dance and sing and lead us to experience, through our own bodies, the joys of movement. Don't ever let anyone tell you that if you are athletically gifted you are automatically a dummy. We are called sentient beings (from the Latin "to feel"). Feel is in everything you do on the mountain, and those adaptive skiers who don't have feeling in their lower legs and can still ski have all the admiration I am capable of giving.

"Your body knows how privileged it is to be here," poet and philosopher John O'Donohue wrote in Anam Cara: A Book of Celtic Wisdom.

Now to other senses. First color. Snow is white because light penetrates and bounces off the ice crystals, and the reflected light contains all colors—which, together, look white. Snow can also look blue, or grey, or purple, or pink depending on the light or shadow. It can also look yellow. Avoid that snow. There is a debate among scholars about how many words Eskimos have for snow. I am not going there.

Ken Wilber in his modestly named book, A Theory of Everything, argues that colors have qualities or characteristics—a kind of dime-store synesthesia where beige is fundamental, red is power, purple is tribal, blue is religious, green sensitive, and so on. If that helps explain the world, bully for you. Coming at color from a different perspective is Michal Levin's Meditation: Path to the Deepest Self, in which she argues that the spirit is not a god out there but a force inside ourselves that our interacting with nature helps to unlock. She writes of blue being peaceful, green harmonious, and red boastful. Others see red and yellow as vitality and power, cheerfulness and wisdom. White is not the absence of color, but the possibility of all colors. There is a theory that soccer goalies in brightly colored uniforms allow fewer goals. I have no evidence, but evidence doesn't seem necessary for proclamations these days.

For me, the monochrome presence of the mountain where the snow is white, the trees are black, and the sky is constantly in flux is what unlocks the pathway to another dimension. It is otherworldly. It is cold and cruel on the one hand, and mysterious and inviting on the other.

We'll watch the architecture
of the clouds create themselves
like flames and disappear like laughter.

—SAMUEL HAZO, "The Quiet Proofs of Love"

The sounds of the mountain are, likewise, engaging, scary, inviting. Wind is the big one. It can be gentle and seductive on a calm day; blustery and demanding on a regular day; or out-of-control angry in a blizzard—defined as at least thirty-five mile per hour winds for three or more hours. Other mountain sounds are the birds, the swish and chatter of your skis (Hemingway captures this), or the boom and reverberation of the patrol throwing charges to dislodge unstable cornices. Snow squeaks under your boot at ten degrees Fahrenheit.

The most compelling sound on the mountain is the silence. The pitches and rhythms in music are framed by what isn't there—the perfectly placed rest that adorns the sound, that allows our ears to catch up, that helps us breathe with the pulses of the earth. Think of the mountain as a cathedral and the wind as the music soaring up to the heavens in praise and thanksgiving.

Smell needs no messenger—it goes from the nose straight to the limbic system—the ancient lizard brain where it can, without thought or interpretation, trigger memories and associations. That is why Realtors who are trying to sell a dog of a house bake gingerbread or cook hot spiced cider during open houses. We can't get away from smell because each of the 23,040 breaths we take each day brings it to us.

Smell is not much associated with skiing except that

years ago there was a doughnut machine in the Mt. Bachelor resort lodge, and that was irresistible. Then there was the Christmas ski trip where, for reasons totally obscure now, we took along our cat. She didn't appreciate the car ride and evacuated her bowels on my ski jacket. I didn't have another, and our cleaning efforts were sufficiently inadequate that the long lift lines were no problem. People gave me lots of space.

The senses transmit nature to us, and from that comes the creative impulse:

> *[...] I shook the habit off*
> *Entirely and forever, and again*
> *In nature's presence stood, as now I stand,*
> *A sensitive being, a creative soul.*
>
> —WILLIAM WORDSWORTH,
> "The Prelude"

Sierra

ALFONSINA STORNI (1892-1938)

Translated from Spanish by Rachel Benson

*An invisible hand
silently caresses
the sad pulp
of the rolling worlds.
Someone, I don't know who,
has steeped my heart
in sweetness.
In the August snow
the blossom of the peach tree—
early flowering—
opens to the sun.
Stretched out on the sierra's
ochre ridge,
a frozen
woman of granite;
the wind howls
the grief of her lonely bosom.
Butterflies
of moon
sip
her frozen
breasts
by night.
And on my eyelids,
a tear swells
older than my body.*

CHAPTER 36

Skiing and the Poetry of Snow

Nature has the right to inflict upon her children the most terrifying jests.

—THORNTON WILDER, playwright

It might seem as if the mountain is just there, inert and shivering, but that would be far from accurate. Snow moves. It settles, it blows, it ripples; it develops a rash of "chicken heads"—those little ice stalagmites that look like, you know, a chicken's head. Snow fractures, drifts, cracks, slumps, and slides. The spring warming and freezing brings corn snow—those ice kernels on the surface with a soft but firm base—ski heaven. And then, also in spring, there is the buttery snow that is soft but carvable until about noon, when it turns into leg-breaking slush.

Ice. Ice defines winter, and there will be plenty of days of it. Sharp edges on the skis are a must as is keeping your weight centered. Sit back and your skis will take off, and you will be on your butt sliding down the ice. Good luck with that one. On a recent day at Bachelor, it was raining at the bottom and ice at the top. A friend on the lift asked when I was going home. "In about twenty minutes." One and done.

It may be that, with global warming, skiing will go the way of glaciers. Becca Jackson, a rowing friend and PhD glaciologist, found that one of her subjects was melting from below 100 times faster than originally thought. Since the dislocations of warming can produce severe weather cycles, it may be feast or famine for established areas, and the unpredictability will make staying economically viable difficult.

Perhaps ski towns can diversify with summer music festivals, mountain slides, mountain biking, and the like. Many already have. But warming can bring persistent drought, blazing summer heat, and forest fires. Poor air quality and vigorous outdoor sports mix poorly, and the legendary Oregon Shakespeare Festival in Ashland had to curtail its outdoor season in summer 2019 because of the threat of heavy smoke (the prior summer, August in particular, was a smoke disaster).

Warmer climes will mean less powder and more wet snow. Snowmaking machines exist in most ski areas, although skiing on manufactured snow just isn't the same. This is true even though snowmaking machines have become more efficient. Squaw Valley's machines are temperature sensitive and can adjust pressure and water volume several times a second to yield 40 percent more snow per gallon of water than they once did. But still, it is a big mountain, and what the most efficient machines can cover is like a narrow fairway on a links golf course. The rest is rocks, roots, and dirt. And it is ugly.

Other climate issues include higher winds, the amount of fossil fuels we exhaust getting to the mountain, and erosion of the slopes. Then there is snowmaking with sewage water. I don't even want to think about it.

CHAPTER 37

Gilgamesh

The man who does not read good books has no advantage over the man who can't read them.

—MARK TWAIN, writer

L et's revisit the oldest story known to humankind, The Epic of Gilgamesh, written in cuneiform (wedge-shaped) script and found in the nineteenth century near Nineveh, once capital of Assyria and now part of Iraq. It predates the Bible and Homer's Iliad by 1,000 years. This story may seem out of place in a book about skiing, but from the earliest writing, comes the theme of humans mistreating the earth. Nothing has changed in that department, and anyway, myth is always appropriate. It is like a sacrament.

Gilgamesh is the tyrant king of the walled city of Uruk. His name means "the old man is a young man," and his powers are superhuman: he does not sleep; his courage and energy are inexhaustible. He is also vain and cruel and selfish, mistreats his subjects (tramples on them like a wild bull), and wants to live forever.

The foil of the story is Enkidu, a peaceful herbivore in human form who lives with and protects the animals in the forest. The tall and magnificent cedar forest is, in turn, protected from humans by the monster Humbaba, who operates at the command of the god Enlil. "You know that this is my place and that I am the forest's guardian," Humbaba says. "Enlil put me here to terrify men…and I guard the forest as Enlil ordains."

Gilgamesh learns about Enkidu and dispatches Shamhat, a sort of sexual high priestess, to bring Enkidu to "civilization"—which she does through a marathon seven straight days of sex and then feeding him human food.

> "Go ahead, Enkidu. This is food,
> We humans eat and drink this." Warily
> He tasted the bread. Then he ate a piece,
> He ate a whole loaf, then ate another,
> He ate until he was full, drank seven
> Pitchers of beer, his heart grew light,
> His face glowed, and he sang out with joy.
> He had his hair cut, he washed, he rubbed
> Sweet oil into his skin, and became
> Fully human.

When Enkidu becomes human, the animals with whom he used to drink at the watering hole run away. But the transformation awakens in Enkidu a longing for human friendship, which he develops with Gilgamesh. Being a vain, selfish tyrant, Gilgamesh decides to enter the forest, subdue the monster Humbaba and cut down a cedar "that is tall enough to make a whirlwind as it falls to the earth." Why do this? "I will make a lasting name for myself, I will stamp my fame on men's minds forever."

Enkidu tries his best to dissuade Gilgamesh, but accompanies him when persuasion fails. When they fight the monster, the winds and natural forces hold Humbaba down to be subdued, but Enkidu is killed. Gilgamesh loses his only friend, but not his quest for immortality, and when he finally chases the sun and obtains the plant that will keep him from ever dying, he leaves it on the bank as he is bathing, a snake comes along, smells its fragrance, and takes it, casting off its skin in the getaway. Upon his return to Uruk, Gilgamesh realizes how beautiful the city is and becomes a better ruler.

How is that for a parable of ambiguity and a demonstration that humankind hasn't changed much over the centuries? It certainly can be read as the first ecological screed—the forest needs protection from humans who will defile it for their selfish purposes. But the wind holds the forest protector down. What's that about? And Gilgamesh gets his friend killed in pursuit of his own vanity. He find his salvation in the plant that will give him eternal life and negligently leaves it where the snake can carry it away (snakes never can catch a break in mythology). Then Gilgamesh seems to wake up to his humanity—sort of—and does a better job of ruling.

Sex is the civilizing force in the story, but it is not at all clear that civilization is civilized. Respect for creation gets lip service but is overrun by human greed and vanity. Religion is lurking in the background, and Gilgamesh's desire to have a godlike life turns out, as most of the other lessons in the tale, ambiguously.

The story is worth remembering, not just because it is a literary masterpiece, but because it displays, from the beginning of history, the tension between preserving and honoring nature, and destroying it. It is the seminal warning, from more than 5,000 years ago, that we must live in balance with nature; that nature needs protection from humankind. In Genesis, the Adam and Eve parable is about humans being in a natural state and in harmony with nature until the snake comes along, and the rest of history is a quest to regain that balance.

In the words of the Don McLean song "Vincent," about the life of artist Vincent van Gogh: "They would not listen / They're not listening still / Perhaps they never will.

Song for the Deer and Myself to Return On

JOY HARJO* (1951-)

This morning when I looked out the roof window
before dawn and a few stars were still caught
in the fragile weft of ebony night
I was overwhelmed. I sang the song Louis taught me:
a song to call the deer in Creek, when hunting,
and I am certainly hunting something as magic as deer
in this city far from the hammock of my mother's belly.
It works, of course, and deer came into this room
and wondered at finding themselves
in a house near downtown Denver.
Now the deer and I are trying to figure out a song
to get them back, to get all of us back,
because if it works, I'm going with them.
And it's too early to call Louis
and nearly too late to go home.

*Poet laureate of the United States, 2019-2020.

CHAPTER 38

John Wesley Powell

Really great men have a curious feeling that the greatness is not in them but through them.

—JOHN RUSKIN, art critic

John Wesley Powell was one of the first Americans to recognize that the southwestern United States was not like the East, the major difference being the lack of water. Powell earned his spurs as a naturalist, an explorer, and a social anthropologist in the years after the Civil War.

He was wounded at the battle of Shiloh, and his arm was removed above the elbow. Here is how the brilliant American writer Wallace Stegner describes Major Powell's reaction: "Losing one's right arm is a misfortune; to some it would be a disaster, to others an excuse. It affected Wes Powell's life about as much as a stone fallen into a swift stream affects the course of the river. With a velocity like his, he simply foamed over it." He did indeed, organizing the first party successfully to float the Grand Canyon, climbing the sheer walls to take geological measurements, overseeing surveys of much of the Southwest, and dealing with a recalcitrant Congress over issues of water, Indian cultures, and preservation of our natural treasures.

The West after the Civil War was the subject of vast hyperbole, wildly inaccurate claims, and romantic nonsense. It was called the New Canaan; a land so moderate in climate that shelter was unnecessary. Three domestic animals could graze where one wild one did, and rain would follow the plow. Settlers didn't need trees on the plains because they could easily dig for and find firewood.

Powell was a realist and a scientist, and he had the inestimable advantage of having walked or floated over the country he was describing. The land beyond the one-hundredth meridian (that which bisects Kansas, Nebraska and Oklahoma) was arid, and the beloved 160-acre homestead plots that had sustained the yeoman farmer in the East were inadequate for settlement of the West. One hundred sixty acres of dry land would not pasture cattle—2,500 acres was needed. One hundred sixty acres of redwood or fir couldn't be made into a homestead, but it was a small fortune. One hundred sixty acres with no access to water would break your back and your heart.

Where others preached unlimited supply and unrestrained exploitation of minerals, land, and resources, Powell counseled conservation, planning, scientific research, mapping, and government stewardship. He wanted lands withdrawn from the public domain to protect them for posterity. He wanted land development to coincide with availability of water, and he foresaw a system of dams and canals to maximize resources. He wanted Indian cultures studied and protected.

As the first public lands director, he fought tenaciously in Washington but lost to the powers of exploitation. Although Yosemite was partially protected in 1864, and Yellowstone

National Park was created by President Ulysses Grant in 1872, it was not until after the turn of the twentieth century, thanks in large part to Theodore Roosevelt, that steps were taken to reduce the carnage of public lands.

I wonder—with our debates and denials of global warming, our overconsumption, and our belief in an endless supply of water—whether we, even we here in the rainy Northwest, are denying John Wesley Powell's prophesies all over again. Science should be persuasive, but with the best science available, Powell lost his noble quest in the nineteenth century, and I fear we will lose ours, much more dramatically, in the twenty-first. As young environmental activist Greta Thunberg says, in these days of coronavirus, we are looking to science to save us, yet we deny science, the clear science, that shows we are killing the earth.

Powell, Wyoming, is named after this great American, and I suppose it is of small consolation to him, being dead and all, but a portrait artist in a local museum there has given him his right arm back.

CHAPTER 39

Abraham's Warning

He has a right to criticize who has the heart to help.
—PRESIDENT ABRAHAM LINCOLN

Democracy is always in the process of becoming. It is dynamic and plastic and is held together, or not, by the actions of its collective citizens. It is, in short, what we make it. Abraham Lincoln shared his thoughts on the glories and perils of democracy in a speech in Springfield, Illinois, on January 27, 1838. This was 23 years before he became president—a time when he was an unknown backwoods lawyer.

After stating that Americans were in possession of a system of government designed to preserve civil and religious liberty previously unknown to history, Lincoln said the task was "gratitude to our fathers, justice to ourselves, duty to posterity, and love for our species in general."

The danger to democracy is not from foreign invasion, he said. "If it ever reaches us, it must spring up among us; it cannot come from abroad. If destruction be our lot we must ourselves be its author and finisher. As a nation of freemen we must live through all time, or die by suicide."

Then, after a description of lawless mob lynchings in both the North and South, Lincoln warned that "the innocent, those who have set their faces against violations of the law in every shape, alike with the guilty fall victims to the ravages of mob law; and thus it goes on, step by step, till all the walls erected for the defense of the persons and property of the individuals are trodden down and disregarded. But all this, even, is not the full extent of the evil. By such examples...going unpunished, the lawless in spirit are encouraged to become lawless in practice; and having used no restraint but dread of punishment, they become absolutely unrestrained. Having regarded government as their deadliest bane, they make a jubilee of the suspension of its operations, and pray for nothing so much as its total annihilation."

After saying that the best of citizens will be alienated by this "mobocratic spirit," he asks: "How shall we fortify against it?" His answer: "Let every American, every lover of liberty, every well-wisher to his posterity swear by the blood of the Revolution never to violate in the least particular the laws of the country and never to tolerate their violation by others...for a man to violate the laws is to trample on the blood of his father and to tear the charter of his own and his children's liberty. Let reverence for the laws be breathed by every American..."

Lincoln continued with a chilling degree of prescience:

The new danger to democracy arises from its success. Men of ambition "aspired to display before an admiring world a practical demonstration of the truth of a proposition which had hitherto been considered...problematical—namely, the capability of a people to govern themselves."

These men succeeded and "won their deathless names in making it so." But "this field of glory is harvested," he said. "New reapers will arise, and they too will seek a field.

"The question then is, can that gratification [for men of ambition and talents] be found in supporting and maintaining an edifice that has been erected by others?" "Most certainly it cannot…Towering genius disdains a beaten path…It scorns to tread in the footsteps of any predecessor, however illustrious. It thirsts and burns for distinction."

Lincoln then asked rhetorically: "Is it unreasonable then, to expect that some man possessed of the loftiest genius, coupled with ambition sufficient to push it to its utmost stretch, will at some time spring up among us? And when such a one does, it will require the people to be united with each other, attached to the government and laws, and generally intelligent, to successfully frustrate his designs."

Further describing such a leader, Lincoln warned: "Distinction will be his paramount object, and although he would as willingly, perhaps more so, acquire it by doing good as harm, yet, that opportunity being past, and nothing left to be done in the way of building up, he would set boldly to the task of pulling down."

Lincoln said that the danger is new because the spirit of the revolution and a common enemy in the form of the British nation had held "the basest principles of our nature… dormant." But with the wounded of the Revolutionary War and the common history "understood alike by the learned and unlearned…gone," a "fortress of strength" has been lost. "They were a forest of giant oaks; but the all-restless hurricane has swept over them and left only here and there a lonely trunk…

"They [that is, our Revolutionaries] were the pillars of the temple of liberty; and now that they have crumbled away that temple must fall unless we, their descendants, supply their places with other pillars, hewn from the solid quarry of sober reason. Passion has helped us, but can do so no more. It will in the future be our enemy. Reason—cold, calculating, unimpassioned reason—must furnish all the materials for our future support and defense. Let those materials be molded into general intelligence, sound morality, and, in particular, reverence for the Constitution and laws…"

I don't want to seem alarmist here, but to quote the Good Book: "He who has ears, let him hear."

In this election year of 2020, with our society in shambles, we need a law-abiding builder because at present we are enduring pretty much what Lincoln feared. As John Milton said: "None can love freedom heartily but good men; the rest love not freedom, but license."

CHAPTER 40

Our National Story

Only Americans can hurt America.
—PRESIDENT DWIGHT D. EISENHOWER

W e don't know who we are as a nation these days. We have misplaced the narrative that tells us how to act in the world.

When the story we inhabit is no longer ours, it becomes a source of strife and confusion rather than guidance. Think about it. Bastion of freedom? We imprison more people than the rest of the world combined. Big shoulders of manufacturing? Gone to China. Moral beacon? Moral countries do not torture. Liberator from tyranny? The rest of the world does not so perceive our massive military might. Functioning democracy? We are screaming at each other, and nobody is listening. Defender of the truth? Truth is in the lost and found. Plus, it seems that political operatives are more than willing to suppress voter turnout to win—hardly a democratic sentiment.

Thomas Jefferson could confidently proclaim: "We hold these truths to be self-evident…" Just what truths do we, as Americans, so hold today? I asked that question in college classrooms across the country, and about all I could determine is that we all have something electronic in our ears and people drive slow in the fast lane.

If we, as a country, stick to the same old story after it is worn out, we are in for a train wreck. But who is in charge of creating a new, vibrant, functioning story? How do we discover what Aristotle called "recognitions"—when we look into our mind's mirror and are surprised by what we see there? How do we catch up to a world moving at warp speed where disinformation is readily and persuasively available?

> *It is difficult*
> *to get the news from poems*
> *yet men die miserably every day*
> *for lack*
> *of what is found there.*
>
> —WILLIAM CARLOS WILLIAMS,
> "Asphodel, That Greeny Flower"

Obviously, no one can dictate our national story: it has to be felt and embraced even if it cannot be exactly articulated. Here are some questions we can ask ourselves, however, to try to re-create the story:

- What do we own, and what are we just borrowing from future generations?

- What is worth dying for?

- What promises will we keep?

- What duties will we acknowledge?

- What sacrifices will we make?

- Is our reason for being on earth to take or to give?

It seems to me that the whole process starts with personal responsibility, and in that sense I admire at least some of those folks who are politically active. I may disagree with most of what they say, but at least they are searching. They are not sitting on their self-satisfied butts and watching, as if democracy were a spectator sport. As Martin Luther King Jr. told us: the opposite of love is not hate; it is indifference.

Political parties "become potent engines by which cunning, ambitious, and unprincipled men...will subvert the power of the people," George Washington warned.

It is time for all patriotic citizens to dump their political party and to register and think independently. The primary aim of both parties is to stay in power, not to do the people's will. George Washington was a seer when he said in 1796 that we should discourage the spirit of parties because "it opens the door to foreign influence and corruption, which finds a facilitated access to the government itself through the channels of party passion." Yup. The Russians have hacked us, and the parties are finger-pointing at each other, but the father of our country is right: the problem is in the whole idea of party. Politics in a democracy requires compromise, a concept totally lost on both major parties.

Neither party has earned our loyalty, and yet we root for them as if they were a football team. Are we incapable of thinking for ourselves? Are we satisfied to watch the daily circus of wrangling and counteraccusation while our health care is a mess, no budget can be passed, one party seeks to undo what the last one did, and our infrastructure crumbles along with our confidence that this country is governable? And the whole country is sick. This can't end well.

The seven deadly sins are lust, envy, covetousness, anger, gluttony, pride and sloth. The mnemonic device for remembering them is: list enumerates character attributes guaranteeing political success. That used to be a joke. Unfortunately, our president owns the whole list in addition to being a serial liar, a misogynist, a cheat, and a blowhard. Can we support him simply because he has hijacked a party label? Do we really think he represents what has been great about America? Is he what we stand for? What we strive for? Is he a role model for our children? And to be realistic, have any of the leaders foisted upon us by political parties earned our trust?

The reform we need is a moral awakening. It starts with the willingness to trust ourselves. Writer F. Scott Fitzgerald put it this way: "Either you think, or else others have to think for you and take power from you, pervert and discipline your natural tastes, civilize and sterilize you." We can gather the facts about most issues. Sure some of them are complex and require experts to guide us, but we should require that they demonstrate expertise, not just political ties.

We can demand that we be told the truth, and we can define truth as that which is verifiable. We can be proud of our country and critical of its missteps. We can vow to do better, to stay involved, to help our neighbors. We have proved that we can shoot each other; can we learn to trust each other and to recognize that the pursuit of happiness in the Declaration of Independence is collective, not individual? Can we, as President John F. Kennedy urged, ask what we can do for our country?

The parties will not willingly cede power. It is up to us, the citizens, to become the caretakers of our country—to take back our right to make collective decisions for the common good, and to re-instill reason, fairness, and compassion as the way we do business. Mark Twain had it right: "Patriotism is supporting your country all the time and your government when it deserves it."

Our national story is not helping us in our most difficult decisions because we are conflicted about its fundamental message. For example, we can make no progress in the health care debate because we do not have a consensus on whether health is a public good or an economic entitlement for those who provide it. Similarly, we keep spending on arms, but we aren't clear as to what constitutes safety, what is domination, and what is simply a gravy train for purveyors of weapons.

We are also conflicted because we can't clearly separate fact from falsehood and because there is so much bullshit flying around, we are cautious at best, and unwilling at worst, to look to intuition and revelation when that sensibility would help or comfort us. Reason is what controls most of our lives. It is what we consult to find the facts; and from the facts, the truth; and from the truth, what we will protect and defend. That is how society functions well, with truth as the cake and a bit of transcendence as the frosting. If it is an upside-down cake, with irrationality as the foundation, then we are well and truly screwed.

Ultimately, a national story that works has to put us in context with the rest of the world, with nature, with a sustainable economy, and a spirituality that transcends what we can see and hold. Maybe we are too angry to accept a story based on reconciliation rather than retribution, but unless we start listening to each other, we will never know.

The truth is in our hearts. Plato knew that: "If I can write the songs of nations, I do not care who writes the laws."

I owe you, the reader, an explanation of how a book examining the internal phenomenon of skiing and its window into the transcendental ends in a screed about abusing the earth, our freedom, and our way of life. In my mind, the transition is both logical and emotional

Our transcendent experience reconnects us with nature. Our reason tells us we are blowing it by destroying the planet and selfishly accepting irrational, foolish, and destructive governance. Our emotions, our love, our humanity plead not just that we do better but that we dedicate ourselves to regaining our societal balance.

It is like the out-of-control skier who, through sheer force of will, refuses to fall and skis out of it.

CHAPTER 41

Thoughts from Corona

We are discussing no small matter,
but how we ought to live.

—SOCRATES IN PLATO'S REPUBLIC

It is April 3, 2020, the coronavirus is racing unchecked through the population, and I haven't been away from the house for a week, except to row my single scull. I've been thinking on what might be different on the other side of this pandemic—thinking of good things, that is. Being isolated and endangered can lead to elevated awareness, just like peak experiences. And it is the very essence of the future to be dangerous, but also to provide opportunity. So here is my list. It is a longing, really.

1. We might, as both a greeting and a sign of respect, bow instead of shaking hands. Shaking hands started as a way to show that one held no weapon. Bowing is an acknowledgement of the other, and it can be to a room, or a person, or any other thing to which we are grateful.

2. We might recognize that we really are all in this together. Corona doesn't respect social status, economic power, or who your parents were.

3. We might appreciate the character and courage of those who have sacrificed for us.

4. We might better appreciate the restorative and mysterious powers of nature. We can take walks, listen to the birds, pick up trash, watch the leaves come out.

5. We might appreciate just talking to each other and losing track of time.

6. We might not always be in a hurry.

7. We might not have to use our cars to get work done.

8. We might reclaim the word righteous as a person, with or without religion, who does the right thing for the right reason.

9. We might appreciate the healing and joyous power of music, particularly singing together even if we have to do it remotely.

10. We might look to the wisdom of indigenous and oppressed cultures. They have been through this before.

11. We might allow reverence and gratefulness to grace our minds and lips.

12. We might think first of kindness rather than criticism.

13. We might learn to be humble.

14. We might atone for our shortcomings, not just those in the past, but for our daily failures and derelictions.

15. We might demand that politics be linked to virtue— real, demonstrated virtue, not political-speak.

16. We might demand and require excellence in all that we buy. No plastic crap; no made-to-fail products.

17. We might listen to our emotions. The tears at a beautiful poem or song tell us what we value.

18. We might acknowledge that it is no weakness to change one's mind.

19. We might choose just to listen for a day. Or longer.

20. We might make a commitment to service.

21. We might decide to own only that which we cannot share, and share the rest.

22. We might relearn the meaning of the words empathy and compassion.

We might.

CHAPTER 42

Coda for Amy

"[I must do] all I can do to help others find peace."

—AMY FROHNMAYER WINN

Some of the recurring themes over these pages have been celebration, courage, knowledge of one's body, coping with loss, appreciating a sense of place, and respecting nature. One who embraced these values with a radiating life force was my niece, Amy.

As I grow older,
I am understanding
With inescapable
Clarity that my life,
As with any life,
Will never be
Devoid of loss
And pain.
My heart has
Broken so
Many times
That I have

Found no
Other choice
But to soften in
Response to the
Painful things—
To accept them
As darkness that
Completes the palette
Of an unbelievably
Colorful life.

—AMY FROHNMAYER WINN

Amy Frohnmayer Winn died in the autumn of 2016 at age twenty-nine.

More alive than anyone I have known, Amy realized, from her earliest understanding, that her life could be truncated by Fanconi anemia—a genetic disease for which there is no known cure. To some, the disease would have been a curse; to her it was an invitation to live with joy and determination and courage and selflessness. She would start to dance the minute the song began. She organized the women's cross-country ski team at South Eugene High School when none of its new members had Nordic skied, let alone raced, before. She graduated from Stanford and took a master's degree in counseling so she could help others who had childhood diseases. She became so proficient a Nordic skier that she would practically float uphill. She ran a marathon. She delighted in decorating the cheese and crackers with pimentos.

She isn't gone. She left an aura—a mystic bond—that inspires those of us who knew and loved her. All of us are amateurs at life, but we can learn from those who live it well, and she was the best at that. When bedridden in her final days and unable to dance, she would do a joyful hand jive while we sang.

> *There are moments*
> *Especially when early*
> *Fall leaves turn fiery*
> *Red, apples come into*
> *Season, and the early*
> *Morning chill calls*
> *For scarves and warm*
> *Drinks, when I'm simply*
> *Compelled to stop*
> *And breathe in the*
> *Awe of being alive.*

—AMY FROHNMAYER WINN

Alex Winn, a remarkable human being, came into Amy's life by a chance meeting at Noi Restaurant in Bend. Alex was looking at dogs on his phone, and that precipitated a three-hour conversation from which they emerged mutually smitten.

As their relationship deepened, and knowing that they had fallen in love, Amy felt compelled to tell him of her medical condition and its life-amending prospects. His response: "That is what makes you so special." Their wedding was set for October 2016, but that May, Amy's body rebelled. They were married in her hospital room in Minnesota, where she had a bone marrow transplant. The transplant failed. Oregon Health & Science University in

Portland then undertook heroic measures. Which failed. To the last she would debate the meaning of the lyrics of Gordon Lightfoot's "If You Could Read My Mind" and ask us to sing it again.

> *I will never*
> *Be able to*
> *Control*
> *All of the music...*
> *I am simply*
> *Learning*
> *How to*
> *Dance this*
> *Life with*
> *A little*
> *More grace.*

> —AMY FROHNMAYER WINN

Loss can be the midwife of inspiration.

The Last Invocation

WALT WHITMAN (1819-1892)

At the last, tenderly,
From the walls of the powerful fortress'd house,
From the clasp of the knitted locks, from the keep of the
well-closed doors,
Let me be wafted.
Let me glide noiselessly forth;
With the key of softness unlock the locks—with a whisper,
Set ope the doors O soul.
Tenderly—be not impatient,
(Strong is your hold O mortal flesh,
Strong is your hold O love.)

JOHN FROHNMAYER .

Appendix A

This is the letter I wrote to myself in March 2020:

I don't know what this book is about. I thought I did when I started. It was to be the last of a trilogy of books about sport and philosophy—the first being Socrates the Rower; the second, Carrying the Clubs: What Golf Teaches Us About Ethics; and then this one on skiing and mysticism. I would look at the instances when, confronted with nature and the speed and grace of the sport, we see outside our earthly boundaries. A fool's errand said my saner self. Words don't work for what you are envisioning.

But poetry, I thought. Poetry is the best words in the best order. It is philosophy condensed; it can communicate before it is understood. I will intersperse poems with the reflections from the slopes and the backcountry skiers, and some thoughtful life-lessons will emerge. That idea is still hanging around.

Next, I thought that maybe this book is about saving the earth—not that a book, and certainly not my book, could do that. But it might just put a finger on the scale toward less plastic and more walking and fewer cars and a lifestyle of care and responsibility. Lots of stories and examples from the snow would apply, but, alas, not all of them on the right side of the scales. Maybe it is the good guys of the backcountry against the flashy city types on the downhill. Simplistic and not entirely true, and I don't want to go there.

Well, then, how about a reflection on the American mind using skiing as the metaphor? There are plenty of juxtapositions and thought disconnects and brain farts I could muster. The American mind, such as it is, may well be on holiday, and some of those brainless wonders are probably skiing. What to make of that? Is there something as singular as an American mind? If there were, is it a good idea to let it out of its cage? If I could lasso it, what would I do with it? Would it drag me around the arena at the end of the rope to the delight of the crowd?

Then came the coronavirus that has locked us all down and scared the shit out of all but the religious congregations in Louisiana who trust God over science and essentially dare God to kill them, and the worshipers of Fox who will exercise their God-given right to ride a golf cart together because it is all a hoax perpetrated by the Chinese, or the Democrats, or the Democratic Chinese. People are dying, and federal leadership is an oxymoron. Trump will be Trump, which means that the rest of us are on our own. Should this book be about what we do on the other side of Corona? Could we listen to Abraham Lincoln who in 1862, while the Civil War raged said: "The dogmas of the quiet past are inadequate for the stormy present…We must think anew and act anew…We must disenthrall ourselves and then we will save our country"?

Disenthrall is a wonderful word. It means jettisoning our ditty bag of prejudices and preconceptions and beliefs and trying to really see the problem and work toward the solution. We need to have a moral debate about values. Leave the politics out for now. Morality is about agreeing on what we want to happen—how we want to live, and how we are willing to treat each other. We are unequipped for the moral debate because we look at every issue first and foremost as being political. That gets us exactly nowhere. When administrations and political power shifts, the new one does its best to disassemble what the one before did. That is not progress. It is stupidity; vainglorious, flaming, dork-headed stupidity, and we tolerate it as if we didn't know better. Our brains welcome what sixteenth-century thinker Teresa of Avila called "idiots in our house."

However this book turns out, it will be about nature. Not sitting, as did Buddha, under the bodhi tree for seven years waiting for enlightenment, but realizing that we are a part of nature, not apart from it. Disappearing into nature is different from being lost in the woods. It is the kind of epiphany we can experience in skiing that transforms knowledge into understanding.

We have got to try. So whatever this book turns out to be, it is my puny voice pleading for sanity in our world, love among our neighbors, and respect for this fragile planet. Good luck in all that.

Appendix B

This is the letter to the editor that I wrote and was published in the *Corvallis Gazette Times* and the *Albany Democrat Herald* on April 3, 2020:

An opportunity to start fresh...

Faced with the Civil War and the potential dissolution of the Union, Abraham Lincoln said: "The dogmas of the quiet past are inadequate for the stormy present...We must think anew and act anew...We must disenthrall ourselves and then we will save our country."

The COVID-19 virus is our generation's challenge, a challenge for which we were and are unprepared, either adequately to fight it or to imagine how this all will come out. But, as with every crisis there comes opportunity. We should have a moral debate about how we wish our country to look and act on the other side of this crisis. A moral debate examines how we wish to live our lives. A political debate (which we have more than enough of) is about winning.

To do this we will, in Lincoln's words, have to disenthrall ourselves, that is put aside the bag of beliefs and prejudices we all have, and talk honestly and respectfully to each other. And listen. Here are some questions we might address:

1. Are we, individually and collectively, willing to sacrifice? If so, for what?

2. If we could change just one thing for the better in our country, what would it be?

3. What responsibility do our elected officials and those in news and other public positions have to tell us the truth?

4. Are we at a point where we can't agree on what is true and what is not?

5. Are we happy about our hostile society where we sling insults and pejoratives at each other?

6. What can we do to make our education system better?

7. Are we a nation of laws, or does the law favor some over others?

8. Is our only choice with COVID-19 to save the economy or to save lives? Is it like war where there are "acceptable losses"?

Here are some thoughts to keep in mind during the discussion: a) Virtually every moral system, at least in the history of the Western world, is based on some iteration of the golden rule—do onto others as you would have them do unto you, or, what is good for me must also be good for all humankind; b) on the other hand, some people just want to be left alone; c) all are entitled to individual dignity; d) the pursuit of happiness in the Declaration of Independence is a collective, not individual pursuit, and yet some see any government action as an infringement on their liberty.

This debate could happen electronically in as many segments as are productive. Perhaps this newspaper could even sponsor them. I have no illusions that we will all end up singing "Kumbaya," but we might learn something about each other and ourselves.

John Frohnmayer lives in Albany. He was chairman of the National Endowment for the Arts during the first Bush administration.

Appendix C

This is the letter I wrote to Oregon Gov. Kate Brown on April 14, 2020:

Hon. Kate Brown, Governor
Office of the Governor
900 Court Street, Suite 254
Salem, Oregon 97301-4047
Re: Declaration of need for statewide health coverage

Dear Governor Brown:

The coronavirus pandemic has added a sense of life or death urgency to the work of the SB 770 task force considering health care for all in Oregon in at least the following ways:

a. Anyone who doesn't have access to care is a threat to spread the disease to others;

b. Private providers such as the Corvallis Clinic are in severe financial difficulty (front page article on this in the Corvallis and Albany papers this morning);

c. Many who had employer sponsored health insurance are no longer employed;

d. Insurance companies often deny or exclude coverage, and in a pandemic there is no time to litigate;

e. Statewide coordination is necessary to share limited resources and to plan for future catastrophic events.

I urge you to use your emergency powers, your powers as Commander in Chief of the Military Department, and your substantial and effective powers of persuasion and leadership to declare that universal health care is a present reality for Oregonians and that there is no time to waste in making it permanent.

The cost the state has and will continue to bear in treatment of this pandemic and the cost of uncompensated care borne by private providers demonstrate that we can and must afford the cost. The moral imperative to treat all of us compels it.

My best personal regards and admiration for the splendid job you are doing in the worst of times.

Sincerely,
John Frohnmayer

Made in the USA
Las Vegas, NV
22 February 2021

18329761R00125